# Better Questioning for Better Learning

T0386158

Learn how to ask deeper questions and develop better questioning habits with this important resource. Author Benjamin Stewart Johnson takes you step by step through the key considerations and brain-based research to keep in mind when developing questions. He begins with an overview of why it's important to understand participants' thought process when being asked questions. He then shows how to set expectations for virtual questions and face-to-face questions; how to plan authentic, higher-order questions; how to scaffold and differentiate questions; and how to avoid zombie questions. In addition, he debunks myths such as wait time and points out the best ways to help learners support their answers, use questions to check for understanding, and more. Each section concludes by helping you create an action plan to improve your skills in a given area. Appropriate for teachers, instructional coaches, training facilitators, and specialists, the book can be used independently or in schoolwide book studies to help educators of all subjects and grades improve the depth and quality of their questioning.

**Benjamin Stewart Johnson** is an educational leader and change agent with a mission to help learners learn more by increasing teacher and administrator effectiveness. As Assistant Superintendent, he turned around a school district from being rated Unacceptable to being rated Recognized by the Texas Education Agency in only three years. He has mentored and coached multitudes of school instructional leaders to increase student learning throughout the state of Texas.

# Better Questioning for Better Learning

## Strategies for Engaged Thinking

Benjamin Stewart Johnson

Routledge
Taylor & Francis Group

NEW YORK AND LONDON

First published 2022
by Routledge
605 Third Avenue, New York, NY 10158

and by Routledge
2 Park Square, Milton Park, Abingdon, Oxon, OX14 4RN

*Routledge is an imprint of the Taylor & Francis Group, an informa business*

*Library of Congress Cataloging-in-Publication Data*
A catalog record for this book has been requested

ISBN: 978-1-032-00786-1 (hbk)
ISBN: 978-0-367-76105-9 (pbk)
ISBN: 978-1-003-17567-4 (ebk)

Typeset in Palatino
by Apex CoVantage, LLC

This book is dedicated to my parents, Robert and Barbara Johnson, who, through their amazing examples, taught me to be curious about the world, to think deeply, and to ask questions to learn about anything and everything.

# Contents

# Acknowledgments

First of all, I thank my editor, Lauren Davis at Taylor and Francis, for being enthusiastic and supporting my writing career. Her encouragement has given me the impetus to complete this book and my other books, and it is my honor to work with her and the fine folks at Routledge, Taylor and Francis, and Eye On Education.

In my research and learning about how humans learn, I must acknowledge considerable dependence on the ideas and thoughts of other individuals. While I have included references for each chapter, there are two particular individuals who deserve to be mentioned. I thank Dr. Daniel Willingham for his insights into how students learn. Reading his book "Why Don't Students Like School?" opened my mind up to the importance of providing learning opportunities that coincide with how the brain works. I thank Dr. Art Costa whose writing inspired me to make asking questions a powerful tool for learning.

Finally, I acknowledge and appreciate the support and encouragement of my darling wife Melanie, without whom this book would never have been attempted. Her patience and her uplifting words sustained me in the long hours of putting my thoughts and ideas into this book.

# Meet the Author

Dr. Benjamin Stewart Johnson is a practical educator who, in a no-nonsense way, tells it like it is in all of his writings on Edutopia. org, his articles, books, and LearningCraft. com. He centers his thinking on what works to increase student learning and builds logical arguments, supported by research and best practices to make it happen. He considers himself a constructivist, which means that he believes that no human being, computer program, or artificial intelligence can impose learning on another. He believes that all learning comes at the consent of the learner and that, for maximum learning, the learner has to passionately desire to learn. Dr. Johnson maintains that the role of educators must change from purveyors of knowledge and skills to motivators and enticers capable of building that passionate desire to learn. His chosen specialty of teaching Spanish aligns perfectly with his philosophy and serves as a foundation for his unique perspective on learning.

Dr. Johnson came to this philosophy from his extensive experience in every realm of education. He has taught nearly every subject to nearly every grade level. He has even taught university education courses online. He has served in small schools and school districts, as well as mega schools and school districts. He has guided charters and regular public schools. He has consulted, trained, and professionally developed teachers and administrators in public schools and colleges and even US Army personnel. He has turned around schools and school systems from failing and has inspired a focus on learning and effective teaching in hundreds of teachers and administrators.

Dr. Johnson's writings on Edutopia.org follow his career and document his hands-on learning techniques over the course of a decade of service. He displays clearly his focus on "learning for a purpose" in the two editions of his book, "Teaching Students to Dig Deeper," where he provides strategies and techniques that instructors of all ages can use to develop ten essential college and career-readiness traits in their learners.

Dr. Johnson has established LearningCraft.com as a repository of learning strategies and techniques for instructors and parents to improve the effectiveness of their instruction and their participants' learning. He welcomes comments and questions. He enjoys living in La Ceiba, Honduras with his beautiful wife and loves to spend time with his children and grandchildren. He is an avid reader and writer of science fiction and spends time long-distance swimming, gardening, woodworking, and tinkering.

To stay in touch with Dr. Johnson, sign up for his weekly newsletters at Learningcraft.com.

# Foreword

## Better Questioning for Better Learning

One of the reasons that we agreed to contribute the foreword to this book is because we share this aspiration: "To make the world a more thought-full place." When we say "thoughtful" we mean both caring and full of thought. And that's what this book is about—making our curriculum and instruction, schools, classrooms, and communities even more full of thought. We want learners to learn how to develop a critical stance with their work, inquiring, editing, thinking flexibly, and learning from one another's perspectives.

We always appreciate and learn most from authors who have a sound philosophy, a vast storehouse of knowledge, and years of practical classroom experience in a variety of settings, all based in tested psychological theory, who can turn that into something practical we make use of in our classrooms. Benjamin Stewart Johnson does just that in this valuable guidebook for proving questioning.

## A Journey Toward Better Questioning and Better Learning

Careful, intentional, productive questioning is one of the most powerful tools skillful teachers possess. Perfecting these tools requires deep thought and intensive practice, and that takes time and effort. Over time, we explore and can deepen our understanding of questioning strategies and become more attuned to opportunities for posing powerful questions. As we continue on the journey of becoming more skillful, strategic, and critically self-reflective of our own questioning, we recognize the value that it brings to deepening learning for our participants and we work to continuously improve, realizing that learning to plan and pose more powerful questions is always a work in progress.

## Awareness

For any educator wishing to improve their classroom questioning, a first step is greater consciousness about their questions and their classroom interaction. Noticing is key. Observing our own questions, thoughts, and behaviors as well as those of others enables us to make wiser, more significant decisions in the moment. We learn to distinguish between those questions that engage and challenge the mind and those that are rhetorical ("zombie questions"). We realize that organizing our questioning strategies by scaffolding them, progressing from data acquisition through processing and elaborating the questions, and then transferring and applying those questions to other situations creates a progression that yields richer responses and creative applications.

### Skill Building

Over time, we explore and deepen our understanding of questioning types, strategies, progressions, and scaffolds. We become more skillful and strategic in our selection and execution of powerful questions.

We analyze the questions we are asking and focus on the syntax and language of the question we are posing. We anticipate the desired type of thinking we are wanting learners to experience and the type of response we are expecting from participants. We, in turn, continue to probe and shape the conversation as we respond in such ways as to deepen their responses.

### Valuing

Soon, we begin to realize the values and benefits of our efforts to improve our questioning. We notice that participants are more engaged, more confident, and more deliberate in their own questioning. We see a wider range of learners who are active participants in the challenges we present. They are posing deeper and more complex questions in their own interactions and dialogs. Their responses to questions become more complex. They volunteer their responses more readily and share what new questions intrigue them. They apply their newly acquired questioning strategies in a wider range of subject areas and situations in school and beyond.

### Advocating

As we recognize the effects of our deeper, more thoughtful, and complex questioning, we become advocates for their use. For example, during a faculty meeting with a complex agenda, we may start problem solving by surfacing questions about that problem before beginning to resolve it. When in a difficult conversation, we may pose questions to invite thinking and feelings about what makes the topic personally controversial. The culture of the entire school community becomes one that promotes inquisitiveness, truth seeking, a thirst for knowledge, and wonderment. As we recognize the effects of powerful, deliberate, thought-provoking questions, we become advocates for their use.

### Commitment

As continuous learners, we constantly strive to improve our craft. Skillful classroom questioning can mature into more than just sets of learned behaviors and becomes more like a mindset. The questioning strategies described in this book pave the way for a journey toward a questioning mindset in which we require no prompting to raise questions. Raising questions becomes an "internal compass" to guide our actions, decisions, and thoughts. When confronted with complex decisions, we ask ourselves,

> What is the most compassionate action I can take right now? What strategies do I have at my disposal that could benefit others? Who else do I need to think about? What intrigues me about this situation and how might I learn from it? How might I use this opportunity to reaffirm my pledge for justice, dignity, hope and love?

As educators, we have a multiplying effect in that our learners become ambassadors of our values. After graduation, participants go forth into the world and apply what they have learned in their work, their communities, and their families. With better questioning, our participants become ambassadors of inquiry, curiosity, and thoughtfulness. It is through them that the world becomes a better, more thoughtful place.

---

Arthur L. Costa, Ed.D. Co- director, Bena Kallick, Ph.D., Co-director
Granite Bay, CA Institute for Habits of Mind Westport, CT

---

# Introduction to *Better Questioning for Better Learning*

I hope as you read this book you will be motivated to reexamine your classroom questioning practices and gain new strategies for effective questions. I also hope that you will start replacing the standby "whole-class" questions with questions that engage all learners in every question.

Trainers,

As you read these chapters, you will learn how to help your instructors to see questions as vital tools to increase participant learning by getting them to start thinking in the right way. In these pages you will discover that the real point of asking questions is not for the teacher to gauge participant learning. It is to get the mental machinery of the learners in high gear. In this book your instructors will learn to engage the participants' brains and bodies, simply by asking effective questions.

Good Luck and Good Questioning,

Dr. Benjamin Stewart Johnson

# Questioning Skills Inventory

| | Questioning Skill | Need Info | Rarely | Some | Often | Chpt |
|---|---|---|---|---|---|---|
| 1 | I avoid using the question "Any questions?" | | | | | 12 |
| 2 | I mix the types of questions I ask: yes or no, short-answer, or open-ended questions. | | | | | 8 |
| 3 | When a learner answers wrong, I ask the question to another learner and then ask the first learner again. | | | | | 17 |
| 4 | I ask questions to learners who don't raise their hands. | | | | | 13.2 |
| 5 | I avoid asking whole-class volunteer questions. | | | | | 2.1, 13 |
| 6 | I ask questions to each of the learners. | | | | | 7 |
| 7 | I ask questions using visual cues to help understanding. | | | | | 8.7 |
| 8 | I scaffold questions to assist struggling learners. | | | | | 9 |
| 9 | I move around the classroom as I ask questions. | | | | | 13.4 |
| 10 | I ask questions with more than one answer. | | | | | 6 |
| 11 | I model effective questioning skills for my participants. | | | | | 5 |
| 12 | I ask substantive questions and expect substantive responses. | | | | | 5 |
| 13 | When I ask questions, I use "wait time" before calling on someone. | | | | | 13.2 |
| 14 | When I ask questions, I use "wait time" before expecting an answer once a learner has been selected. | | | | | 13.2 |
| 15 | I do not prefer one group of learners over others. | | | | | 8.6 |

| | Questioning Skill | Need Info | Rarely | Some | Often | Chpt |
|---|---|---|---|---|---|---|
| 16 | I organize the class so every learner has a voice in discussion. | | | | | 6 |
| 17 | I have a system to not ask the same participant questions all the time. | | | | | 13.3 |
| 18 | I teach learners how to ask questions. | | | | | 14 |
| 19 | I teach learners how to answer questions. | | | | | 14 |
| 20 | I expect every learner to answer the question in some form. | | | | | 13.4 |
| 21 | I use different grouping opportunities so everyone can answer a question. | | | | | 7 |
| 22 | I have learners all answer the question at the same time. | | | | | 13.2 |
| 23 | I have learners physically respond to questions. | | | | | 13.4 |
| 24 | I write, say, and visually represent each question. | | | | | 8.7 |
| 25 | I tier questions according to difficulty and complexity. | | | | | 8.2 |
| 26 | When I create my lesson plans, I also create a list of questions I want all learners to be able to answer. | | | | | 6 |
| 27 | I adjust my questions to account for different cultures. | | | | | 8.7 |
| 28 | I prepare questions targeted to particular learners based on their needs and interests. | | | | | 7 |
| 29 | I prepare questions that engage each learner in the class. | | | | | 6, 7 |
| 30 | I prepare questions with several unknowns or parts. | | | | | 5 |
| 31 | I prepare questions concerning current concepts and foundational concepts. | | | | | 15 |
| 32 | I prepare questions concerning principles. | | | | | 6 |
| 33 | I prepare a few convergent questions. | | | | | 6 |

| | Questioning Skill | Need Info | Rarely | Some | Often | Chpt |
|---|---|---|---|---|---|---|
| 34 | I prepare advanced divergent questions. | | | | | 6 |
| 35 | I prepare learners to be successful in inquiry learning. | | | | | 14 |
| 36 | I align questions with learner skills and interests in mind. | | | | | 7 |
| 37 | I ask knowledge and comprehension questions to prepare for advanced questions. | | | | | 10 |
| 38 | I ask critical-thinking questions for learners to evaluate value. | | | | | 5 |
| 39 | I ask problem-solving questions for learners create solutions. | | | | | 5 |
| 40 | I answer questions from learners with questions to probe their understanding further. | | | | | 14 |
| 41 | I ask questions to teach. | | | | | 13.3 |
| 42 | I ask questions to assess. | | | | | 16 |
| 43 | I ask questions to motivate. | | | | | 15 |
| 44 | I ask questions to get learners to think. | | | | | 12 |
| 45 | I ask questions to get learners to apply knowledge. | | | | | 3.2 |
| 46 | I ask questions showing positive regard. | | | | | 8.4 |
| 47 | The questions I pose to learners are the same questions on the evaluations. | | | | | 20 |
| 48 | I prepare questions to inspire curiosity. | | | | | 14 |
| | Total for questions 1–12 (skill in asking) | | | | | |
| | Total for questions 13–24 (skill in engagement) | | | | | |
| | Total for questions 25–36 (skill in planning) | | | | | |
| | Total for questions 37–48 (skill in choosing a purpose) | | | | | |

# Section I

## Questioning Foundation

In this section you will find a different perspective on asking questions than what you might be expecting. I did an internet image search of the word "teacher" and got 30 pictures of teachers in the classroom. What I found amazing was that of those 30 pictures, 28 of them depicted teachers standing in the front of the room, in front of a whiteboard and chalkboard pointing or lecturing. Only two pictures illustrated teachers among the students providing assistance directly. Because of this pervasive notion of what a "teacher" does, I have chosen to not use the word "teacher" or even "student" for the same stereotypical reasons.

Unfortunately, this lopsided perspective of the traditional "teacher" is prevalent among many practicing instructors as well. This is demonstrated in how instructors in all educational endeavors ask questions in much the same way: whole-group questions. A theme of this chapter (and this book), or you may consider it all-out war, is the abolition of the traditional "whole-group" questioning. The theory behind this effort to eradicate "whole-group" questions is that in asking such a question the expectation is that only one learner at a time can answer, but the assumption that all the other participants are listening and learning at the maximum level is false. You will see that I propose a different expectation: if the question is worth asking, then all the learners need to answer some form of the question not just once but multiple times.

# 1

## Questions

### Why Ask Questions?

Most of what we currently consider "teaching" revolves around asking questions to participants. The current priority of questions is revealed in the fact that at least 80% of what an instructor does is ask questions.[1] In the course of typical lessons, teachers ask from 30 to 120 questions per hour or 300 to 400 questions per day.[2] But even though many questions are asked, data shows that typical questioning strategies employed in schools and colleges today are ineffective in increasing participant learning.[3] Researchers have scratched their heads about this for decades. Various studies have discovered some possible reasons for this anomaly: the level of the questions' rigor is insufficient, the purpose of the questions is off target, the methods of asking the questions are inadequate, and/or the teachers simply are not experienced enough.[4] In this book we will discover the "why's" and "why for's" of all of the above.

## 1.1 The Purpose of Asking Questions

Let's begin this discussion about questions by asking a question. Why do instructors ask questions? Well, for the most part, it's tradition. Ever since Socrates and earlier, educators have been asking questions. We are all familiar with the Socratic method (right?).[5] But even more than this, somehow, it just does not feel like "teaching" if the instructor is not drilling learners with questions. Over the years, educators' perceptions of why they ask questions has changed as the educational climate has changed—but not as much as you might expect. In 1967 a survey of 190 teachers was performed, later repeated in 1987 with 20 teachers, and then again in 2007 with 86 teachers. In all three surveys teachers were asked only one question: "what are three important purposes of teachers' questions of pupils?"[6] Based on the teacher's prioritized responses to this question, the researchers were able to identify, across a 40-year span, a 9% decrease in the importance of "assessment-type" questions and a 19% decrease in the importance of "teacher-type" questions (questions that check on the effectiveness of teaching). In that same 40-year spread, there was noted a 14% increase in "thinking-type" questions that was matched by the same percentage increase in "motivation-type" questions (questions that discover a learner's interests)[7] (see Figure 1.1). The year 2007 compared to 1987 shows an interesting trend that I witnessed in my teaching career. In 1987 there was more of an emphasis on motivation than thinking, and in 2007, motivation is just slightly higher than thinking. This is good news! It indicates a trend that instructors are starting to adjust their reasons for using questions toward engaging learners' own desires to learn and using questions to help them reach higher cognitive levels (in Chapter 3 we will visit this idea in more detail). The following is a graphical representation of the data from these three studies.

## 1.2  Gap in Questioning

Over these 40 years in education, as you would imagine, significant changes for the better took place in pedagogical strategies and teaching methodologies. We went from the stoic Sputnik-inspired programmed learning, to

Figure 1.1  Percent of Responses of Experienced Teachers

metacognition and connected learning, and finally to brain-based learning. Some of these could account for the shifts in perceptions shown in the
previous data. Even still, one would think that in 2007—and even today—
higher-order thinking would hold a more prominent position in the minds
of the instructors. Admittedly, the perceptions of the teachers in the three
previous studies were self-reported, and no correlation was made to what
those teachers actually did in the classrooms, but if thinking is still number
three in the list of priorities for asking questions, then we cannot expect
that the actual frequency of "thinking" questions would be greater. This
is in fact corroborated by other research data, as we will see. A significant
gap exists between what instructors perceive as important uses of questioning and how instructors actually use questioning in the classroom.
For example, even though Bloom's Taxonomy has been around since 1956,
the overwhelming majority (from 60% to 79%) of questions asked in most
classrooms are of the lowest levels: knowledge and comprehension level
questions.[8] Over the years (1956–2002), other researchers have corroborated
this same data, and it seems to hold steady.[9] In the previously mentioned
research, teachers believed that 32% of all questions should be thinking/
teaching questions, but in looking at data regarding actual question fre-
quencies, teachers ask only 20% thinking/teaching questions. This is a 12%
gap between how often teachers believe they should ask thinking questions
and how often they actually do ask thinking questions. The gap is larger
(30%) when you consider that at least 50% of questions posed to learners
should be higher-order thinking questions[10] When actual questions asked
in the classroom are broken down into productive (Bloom's Analysis, Synthesis or Evaluation) questions and reproductive (knowledge and comprehension) questions, the gap is more apparent. In a 2009 study by Tienken,
Goldberg, and DeRocco, 98 teachers were observed, and out of all the questions asked, only 24% of them were productive (see Figure 1.2). Experienced
teachers reduced the gap by asking 32% productive questions compared to
the novice teachers at 15%.

In the same study, Tienken et al. give the following analogy,

Lawyers learn to treat their questioning strategy as akin to cartogra-
phy. Just as a cartographer plots out on a map the route to a destina-
tion, attorneys develop a sequence of questions, ahead of time, to lead
their clients to the desired point in the examination. Like lawyers and
cartographers, teachers need to plan a route and strategy in order to
use questions productively and develop students' thinking based on
the learning objectives for their lessons. Just as a lawyer would not
ask questions aimlessly or without a strategic purpose or vision of the

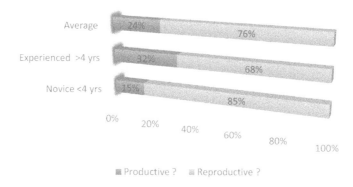

Figure 1.2 2009-grade 3–12 Teachers Frequency of Productive vs Reproductive Questions

big picture, teachers should not leave to chance the development of student critical thinking.[11]

The whole point of this book is to help instructors take on the act of deliberately creating series of questions leading learners to a desired set of knowledge and skills. But the fact that instructors need to improve their questioning capacity is hardly surprising and not new.

Even long before the standardized testing boom, teachers believed that asking questions to assess learning was the highest priority. While the perceptions of why questions should be asked has changed a bit in the 40-year study, it turns out that over the same 40-year period, the number of thinking questions asked has remained the same (see Figure 1.3). In reviewing several research studies across this time period, when classrooms were observed, 80% of the questions were low-level, factual questions, and only 20% were thinking questions.

Since instructors know that higher-order questions increase memory and learning, why do instructors still depend so heavily on low-level questions? Is it that instructors simply do not have the skills or training to be able to bring the learners to higher cognitive levels through questions? Is it that not enough instructors truly believe that the ultimate goal of questioning is to help our learners learn at the highest levels? Or is it both? This is your lucky day. The solution to both of these questions is in your hands at this very minute! It just so happens that the main goal of this book is to help instructors realize the power of questions, gain practical and specific knowledge on how to employ questioning effectively, and understand how to engage all learners with questions.

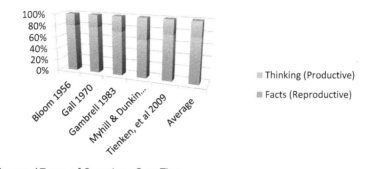

Figure 1.3 Observed Types of Questions Over Time

## Why Ask Questions?

There are quite a number of reasons for asking questions, but they can all be categorized into four areas: assessment, motivation, thinking, and teaching.[12] As mentioned earlier, it should be no surprise that instructors assess learner understanding most often by asking questions using recall and recognition of information and skills. In terms of Bloom's taxonomy, these types of questions are low-level (knowledge and comprehension) and compose more than 80% of the questions experienced instructors typically asked.[13] Although knowledge and comprehension are necessarily the starting point for learning, many instructors never get past that level. Schmoker (2006)[14] cites a study in which 1,500 classrooms were observed, and in those observations, it found that only 3% of them were utilizing higher-order thinking activities, and in 85% of the classrooms, fewer than 50% of the students were actually engaged (p. 18). Schmoker states that teachers should know how to engage students in higher-order thinking, and for the most part, they are capable of engaging students in higher-order thinking, but because of the convenience of isolation, they choose not to employ those skills (p. 25).

Perhaps it really is an issue of the instructors not knowing how to prepare and ask effective questions. Hannel (2009) reports that teachers have a general idea of how to ask questions, but if you asked them to describe their questioning strategy, they lack the detailed knowledge and precision about the process that is characteristic of other teacher duties, such as assessment. They would not be able to explain in any detail the questioning process that they employ, the reasons for it, and the research behind it (p. 66).

## 1.3  Training on Questioning

If 80% of what instructors do is ask questions, then it stands to reason that they should be able to explain how they intend to make the questioning effective. They should be able to identify a definite questioning strategy that covers all areas of the learning cycle—including assessment—and engages a maximum number of learners in that cycle. Instructors should be able to describe their personal philosophy of learning and memory and how they use the questioning cycle to implement it. Instructors should be able to classify the types of questions they asked, the purposes of the questions, and the intended responses. Instructors should also be proficient at scaffolding questions or, in other words, helping learners be successful answering questions, according to difficulty and complexity à la Bloom's. It should be second nature for instructors to identify effective questions that show participant learning gaps. Instructors should also be aware of their biases and preferences when employing questioning and be able to describe their plan to accommodate for them. Because questioning is so integral to the business of teaching and learning, if asked to provide such detail concerning their questioning habits, instructors should be able to provide it. Clearly, some instructors are in need of targeted professional development about asking "highly effective questions,"[15] and every instructor needs a good book (like this one) on how to ask questions effectively so that all learners are engaged and learn at higher levels.

The Learning Cycle (see Figure 1.4):

1  Acquire knowledge
2  Organize and categorize knowledge
3  Apply knowledge
4  Practice—commit to long-term memory
5  Demonstrate knowledge

In the three studies covering 40 years, there were originally 14 different categories of the responses to their research question "What are three important purposes of teachers' questions of pupils?".[16] Wallace and Hurst condensed these reasons for asking questions into four categories: Assessment, Motivation, Thinking, and Teaching. In their study they are listed in order of relative importance according to the teachers surveyed in the study. I believe that the order should be Thinking first, then Teaching, Assessment, and Motivation, which better matches what we know about learner memory and effective and affective learning.[17]

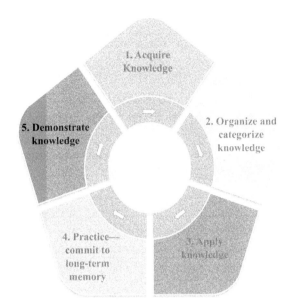

Figure 1.4  *Four Reasons for Asking Questions*

## Thinking

When asking questions for <u>Thinking</u>, the instructor helps learners look at concepts from different perspectives, to compare that what they already know, and then evaluate the value of the new information. Typically, these are true inquiry questions in which the answer really is not known. They are open-ended questions that seek explanations, solutions, and opinions. (Chapter 6 will discuss how instructors can use questions to get learners thinking.)

## Teaching

Asking questions for <u>Teaching</u> purposes typically means the instructor hides the answer to the question within the question and guides or channels learner thoughts through several leading questions. A skilled instructor will be able to scaffold the teaching questions, ones with specific answers, from cognitively simple questions to intellectually complex questions. (Section 8.2 will discuss how instructors can tier questions to teach learners.)

## Assessment

In asking questions for <u>Assessment</u>, the instructor attempts to calculate the level of learning and understanding of the participants, giving the instructor a direction in which to aim further questions. Recall is the major purpose of assessment questions. These questions typically start in the cognitively easy domain but can (if designed properly) evaluate learner understanding at all of Bloom's Taxonomy levels. (Section IV will discuss how instructors can use questions to assess learners.)

## Motivation

Asking questions for <u>Motivation</u>, the instructor endeavors to move learn-ers into action or help them understand their actions. Many classroom management techniques use questions to help learners take responsibility for their actions through reflection. Metacognition is a motivational ques-tioning technique that helps guide learners through the thought processes behind behaviors. Meeting learner needs requires motivation questions. (Chapter 15 will discuss how instructors can use questions to motivate learners.)

## Conclusion

So, to answer the question of this chapter, "Why Ask questions?" it boils down to the following: instructors ask questions to help guide, foment, startle, excite, and motivate learners to learn. There are also many ancillary reasons for asking questions, some that benefit the instructor more than the learner, but participant learning has to be the most important reason to ask questions. Although the Wallace and Hurst categories for why instructors ask questions are not the only set of categories that researchers have used, they are just as good as any other and therefore will be used throughout this book to guide us as we explore effective questioning.[18] The following chapters will further define how these reasons for asking questions correlate to the actual question types and increased participant learning.

## Summary

1  Asking questions is 80% or more of what instructors typically do in the classroom, yet for various reasons, asking questions is not helping partic-ipants learn effectively.

2  Instructors still believe, as they did 40 years ago, that <u>Assessment</u> is the most important reason to ask questions. Asking questions to get learners to think has increased slightly as well as asking questions to improve the quality of teaching.

3  A gap exists between what instructors believe is the priority for ask-ing questions and the patterns of questioning that actually occur in the classroom.

4  Some instructors don't know much about questioning. Because ques-tioning is so vital, instructors should be able to describe in detail the questioning strategies and techniques they use to help participants learn.

5  This book will use the four categories of the reasons for asking questions in prioritized order: Thinking, Teaching, Assessment, and Motivation.

**Questions to Consider**

1   Why do you ask questions of your participants? (check all that apply)
    ◆   To keep them awake?
    ◆   To check and see if they have done their reading?
    ◆   To engage the learners in discussion?
    ◆   Make the class interesting?
    ◆   Tradition?
    ◆   You can't teach without asking questions?
    ◆   Check for understanding?
    ◆   Trick the learners?

2   What is your personal philosophy of learning and memory, and how do you use the questioning cycle to implement it?

_____

_____

3   What types of questions do you ask and why?

_____

_____

4   What kind of answers to those questions would be ideal?

_____

_____

5   How do you scaffold your questions to assist struggling learners?

_____

_____

6   How do you identify effective questions that show participant learning gaps?

_____

_____

7   What biases and preferences do you exhibit when questioning, and can you describe your plan to accommodate for them?

_____

_____

8    What other questioning habits have you noticed in your instruction?

_____

_____

9    What are some ways that you can identify how many questions you ask and what level of questions they are?

_____

_____

10   What do you know about asking questions?

_____

_____

11   According to the results from the questioning inventory that you took, what element of the four purposes for questioning are you going to begin perfecting?

_____

_____

_____

_____

## Notes

 1   (Marzano, 2001, p. 113).
 2   (Tienken, Goldberg, & DiRocco, 2009, p. 40).
 3   (Zhang, Lundeberg, McConnell, Koehler, & Eberhardt, 2010, p. 58).
 4   (Rowe, 1974, 1987; Tienken, Goldberg, & DiRocco, 2009; Albergaria, 2010).
 5   The Socratic method involves asking questions to get to the truth—or at least what is most likely true. This website has a good description of what the Socratic method is and some great examples of questions: https://lifelessons.co/critical-thinking/socratic-method/.
 6   (Wallace & Hurst, 2009, p. 30).
 7   (Wallace & Hurst, 2009, p. 45)?
 8   (Tienken et al., 2009, pp. 41–42).
 9   (Bloom, 1956; Gall, 1970; Gambrell, 1983; Myhill & Dunkin, 2005).
10   (Tienken et al., 2009, p. 42).
11   Ibid.

12 (Wallace & Hurst, 2009, p. 42).
13 (Tienken et al., 2009, p. 42).
14 Schmoker, M (2006) Results Now. Alexandria, Virginia: ASCD.
15 Ibid., p. 69.
16 (Wallace & Hurst, 2009, p. 30).
17 Ibid., p. 42.
18 Ibid.

## References

Albergaria, P. (2010). Questioning patterns, questioning profiles and teaching strategies in secondary education. *International Journal of Learning*, *17*(1), 587–600. doi:10.1504/IJLC.2010.035833

Bloom, B. S. (1956). *Taxonomy of educational objectives, handbook I: The cognitive domain*. New York: David McKay Co Inc.

Gall, M. D. (1970). The use of questions in teaching. *Review of Educational Research*, *40*(5), 707–721. doi:10.3102/00346543040005707

Gambrell, L. B. (1983). The occurrence of think-time during reading comprehension instruction. *Journal of Educational Research*, *77*(2).

Hannel, I. (2009). Insufficient questioning. *Phi Delta Kappan*, *91*(3), 65. Retrieved December 12, 2011, from https://search.ebscohost.com/login.aspx?direct=true&db=f5h&AN=45086096&site=eds-live

Marzano, R., Pickering, D., & Pollock, J. (2001). *Classroom instruction that works: Research-based strategies for increasing student achievement*. Alexandria, VA: Association for Supervision and Curriculum Development.

Myhill, D., & Dunkin, F. (2005). Questioning learning. *Language & Education: An International Journal*, *19*(5), 415–427.

Rowe, M. B. (1974). Wait-time and rewards as instructional variables, their influence on language, logic, and fate control: Part one—Wait-time. *Journal of Research in Science Teaching*, *11*, 81–94.

Rowe, M. B. (1987). Wait time: Slowing down may be a way of speeding up. *American Educator*, *11*, 38–43.

Schmoker, M. (2006). *Results Now: How we can achieve unprecedented improvements in teaching and learning*. Alexandria, VA: Association for Supervision and Curriculum Development.

Tienken, C. H., Goldberg, S., & DiRocco, D. (2009). Questioning the questions. *Kappa Delta Pi Record*, *46*(1), 39–43. Retrieved December 12, 2011, from https://search.ebscohost.com/login.aspx?direct=true&db=ehh&AN=45422447&site=eds-live

Wallace, R., & Hurst, B. (2009). Why do teachers ask questions? Analyzing responses from 1967, 1987, and 2007. *Journal of Reading Education*, 35(1), 39–46. Retrieved December 12, 2011, from http://ehis.ebscohost.com/eds

Zhang, M., Lundeberg, M., McConnell, T. J., Koehler, M. J., & Eberhardt, J. (2010). Using questioning to facilitate discussion of science teaching problems in teacher professional development. *Interdisciplinary Journal of Problem-Based Learning*, 4(1), 57–82. doi:10.1007/s10972-009-9161-8

# 2

# Questioning Perspective

## What Really Happens Inside a Participant's Head When an Instructor Asks Questions?

### 2.1 Participants' Thought Processes in Face-to-Face Learning

A typical learning situation starts with the instructor at the front—or in control of the learning platform online—and a group of associated learners.[1] Information is presented in one form or another, and then an effective next step is to check for understanding. This checking for understanding is usually broadcasted in the form of a question. What goes through the learners' heads when they receive this question? In-person learners have several dynamics already built into the classroom and will be discussed later.

One dynamic is that the most eager learners, if allowed, will sit in the front while the least eager will sit as far from the instructor as possible. Another dynamic is that most questions that instructors give are general questions given to the entire group, requesting volunteers to answer. Those participants who are most interested or most outgoing will volunteer. What are the rest of the learners doing? Do they not volunteer because they do not know the answer and do not want to show their ignorance? Do they not understand, or are they not interested in the question? Do they suffer from lack of self-confidence and are afraid to respond? Do they not want to be arrogant and show that they know the answer? Are they lazy and do not want to be troubled to answer questions that others can answer? Are they even listening to the question? There's no way to know. Each of us has been in a classroom situation and not answered questions for one of those reasons. Some of us habitually never answer questions as a matter of principle. Whatever the reasons for not answering questions are, it is foolish to assume that every person in the learning group is eagerly paying attention and fervently desires to know the answer to the question.

So, the instructor chooses someone to answer the question, usually in the front of the group or the person who is most enthusiastic about answering the question. Instantly, everyone else is off the hook. They feel no pressure to check their own understanding or even listen to the answer if they don't want to. They may listen, but the conversation is now between the instructor and one learner, not the whole group and not them. Some may be listening, but listening is a passive activity, and as you will learn later on, hearing has to compete with a multitude of other sensory inputs, so the information is unlikely to stick in their brains. Experienced instructors will proceed to ask a multitude of similar questions seeking more participation from other volunteers trying not to allow one person to answer all the questions. Typically, however, the learners in the front will monopolize the answering of questions, and those learners in the back will be perfectly happy to let them.

More savvy instructors will begin to ignore the raised hands and ask question of those learners not raising their hands. Consistent application of this technique will increase the likelihood of non-participatory learners paying attention, but it is not a guarantee. Learners in the back are acquainted with multiple techniques to ward off instructors asking questions. Pretending to be doing something else, avoiding eye-contact, dropping a pencil etc. Often, a quick, "I don't know" is all that is needed to get the instructor to go elsewhere. But the problem remains. They are not engaged. In essence the instructor is carrying on a dialogue with one learner while the rest of the learners are supposed to be listening passively.[2]

What happens when a learner goes into "active" mode either by choice or by being called on; what are the other learners in the room doing? Correct! Not much! They go into "passive" mode. In passive mode, the information coming from the instructor conversing with the other learner is easily drowned out by all of the other information passing through the reticular formation into their neocortex (see Section 2.4). Basically, while one learner is answering the question, the other learners' brains are on hold. They may be listening—but not actively—which makes the chance of "learning" or remembering what is said next to nil, and even that little bit diminishes rapidly over a short period of time. As you can see, under the guise of asking questions to the whole class, in reality, asking one learner at a time is a very inefficient way to increase learning opportunities for all the learners. Also, in doing this, the instructor unwittingly sends the message "Your time is not important" to other learners waiting to participate. A learner may think, as

I have on many occasions, "Why do I need to be here if the instructor always talks to the learners in front?"

The other problem is that the instructor is doing most of the work, and the learners are simply existing, waiting for the brilliant instructor to tell them what they need to know. When delivering the carefully constructed questions to the whole class, the instructor assumes that when one learner answers the question that all the others are paying attention to what the instructor is doing, but most likely, the learners not currently engaged with the instructor directly have allowed their attention to lapse in favor of other thinking activities, electronic devices included. This is what happens in 99% of all in-person classrooms, workshops, seminars, and especially lectures. We allow our learners to develop poor learning habits because of the way we consistently ask questions. Keep reading to discover how to fix this.

## 2.2  Participants' Thought Processes in Synchronous Virtual Learning

For synchronous learning where an instructor is directing the learning of a group of learners who are in remote locations, all logged in at the same time as in a video conference, checking for understanding has further ramifications, not the least of which is that the instructor has less control over what the learners may or may not be doing if not listening. The instructor may ask for volunteers to answer questions, and similar scenarios for responding or not responding will exist, with the added excuses of not being familiar with the technology and multitasking. Those most eager will answer all the questions, while the nonrespondents are happy to let them. Savvy instructors will call on nonparticipants to answer questions, but once again, it becomes a conversation between two people, and the rest of the learners are in a holding pattern.

## 2.3  Participants' Thought Processes in Asynchronous Virtual Learning

Asynchronous learning is a style of learning where the participants are given a time range in which to participate with prepared material, usually a written or video lecture and a series of essay questions. The marked advantage that asynchronous learning has over the other two learning situations mentioned previously is that the instructor's only way to judge attendance is that every learner must do something, like answer an instructor's question or comment on other learners' responses, though not at the same time. This forces the learners out of the "passive" mode and into the active mode. Certainly, learners can take the easy path by asking Jeeves or plagiarizing from Google, but even then, they have to find the answers, and something may stick due to their active behavior.

You may feel that the previous examples are somewhat contrived, but I would venture that they are pretty true to form. Now let's discuss what else is happening in the learners' brains when the instructor is trying to engage the learners with questions. To begin with, when learners listen, it is a fairly passive activity most of the time, so any information gained from passive listening has to compete with all of the other things that are vying for the learner's attention.

## 2.4  Engaging the Participants' Brains and the Reticular Formation

The brain is an amazing mechanism. It constantly receives, filters, and categorizes thousands of bits of information per second. Some we choose to pay attention to, while others we are blissfully able to ignore such as autonomous internal body functions; heart rate, breathing, blinking, etc. Then the external sensory organs constantly flood the brain with data like the external temperatures, the touch of the pencil used for doodling, the sound of the air conditioner whirring, the level of light, the smell of the perfume on the girl in front, the feeling of the hard desk chair, a fly buzzing in the window, the tick of the clock on the wall, the sound of the instructor's heartbeat, oh wait . . . that was superman as a boy. Added to this, especially in junior high-aged learners, hormones and emotions, and it's a wonder that we can pay attention to anything at all! The problem we all face is that all of this sensory, hormonal, and emotional input is constantly bombarding the brain at the same time that we expect our learners to be paying attention to our wonderful questions.

Fortunately, the brain has a solution. It is called the reticular formation.[3] It is a part of the brain located just above the spinal cord, at the top of the brain stem, and it acts as a gateway to the brain. It is composed of special nerve cells that allow incredible amounts of connections through special dendrites and synapses. Incredibly, this structure allows us to be able to prioritize information, data, and sensory input coming from the rest of our bodies and allows us to focus on one thing. In other words, it allows us to pay attention to the things we choose. All information coming from the five senses as well as feedback from muscles and the sense of balance flows through the brain stem to this reticular formation. This organ filters this information and provides the ability to "pay attention" or the ability to focus on just part of the overwhelming volumes of information flowing to our brains.

We have all had the experience of being focused on one thing—so much so that we don't hear noises or distractions, we ignore heat or cold, we don't feel hungry or tired. That is the reticular formation doing its job. Has that ever happened to you in a classroom learning situation? In my case, I get super focused in athletic competitions, performances, writing, reading, creating, building, or even playing a video game. Notice any patterns here? It is not passive and is almost always initiated voluntarily!

## 2.5 Getting Learners to Pay Attention

That is the key, then. Getting learners to pay attention. It can't be that hard. All I have to do is say, "Listen up!" or "Write this down, it will be on the quiz." If only it were that easy! Fortunately, what we know about the brain can help. Since we know that attention—or the ability to focus on one thing—is regulated by the reticular formation, what is it that prompts "attention"? I propose that it is a sense of urgency. We look at urgency usually as something negative: "You have to do this now, or something bad will happen." Well, that is our experience, for example with our own bodies. It is amazing how fast we can move when trying to find a restroom. Immediate threats and consequences seem to motivate us most. Future threats and consequences don't usually have the power to make us move immediately unless we have experience where procrastination has been disastrous or if we are of the rare breed that gets things done right away. The motivation has to be urgent to get the learner's attention.

The best attention-getter is simply changing a passive listener to an active participant. In other words, give the learners something to do, like a list of questions that they must ask and record the answers of every participant with blue eyes. Maybe just show the questions on the PowerPoint slide and have them quiz their elbow partner. Or even better, ask "Shakespeare's Macbeth can be most closely related to_____. You have 30 seconds to stand under one of the answers posted on the wall that best matches your thinking." Follow up with this request: "with the people that chose the same answer as you, reach consensus on an answer for each of the questions on the screen. You have 2 minutes." Be aware that most learners are unaccustomed to being active in learning, and it will take an adjustment period and patience.

## 2.6 Developing a Sense of Urgency

The instructor of the class sets the tone and develops a sense of urgency in many ways. Urgency requires a short time limit. It requires that it be important and that it cannot be ignored. It also requires that it be personal. If learners have to do something with the information they receive, it becomes urgent.

I know I always refer back to the arts and athletics, but that is where our thinking should be. In the arts and athletics, learners have to prepare and then demonstrate what they can do in front of an audience. It definitely is time-bound, it is important and cannot be ignored, and their personal reputations are on the line (you can learn more about this if you refer to my book *Teaching Students to Dig Deeper*, Section II p. 109–111).

As in the example I used earlier about Macbeth, if learners have to do something with another learner, that automatically raises the sense of urgency. If the learners know that they will have to present to the group or perform for an audience, that automatically raises the sense of urgency. The other dimension of urgency is importance. Steven R. Covey describes outside motivations in four categories: urgent and important, urgent and not important, not urgent and important, and not urgent and not important.[4] He states that effective people spend most of their time responding to motivations that are not urgent and important. I would like to modify his graph for questioning in the following way: instructors need to create learning opportunities that involve questions that are both urgent and important, urgent meaning that something needs to be done immediately with those questions and important meaning it is worthwhile spending time to answer the questions (see Figure 2.1).

In asynchronous learning, there is no way to make your questions urgent and important. The only questions that you should consider are those that are not urgent (meaning you have some time to answer them) but are still important. Part of being an instructor that seeks to better your questioning skills is taking the time to reflect to see if any of your questions fall into the categories of "urgent but not important" or "not urgent and not important" and then making the necessary corrections.

### Flamboyancy Not Necessary

We all know instructors who get up on top of their desks and read poetry, dress up in civil war uniforms, or perform dramatic scientific experiments

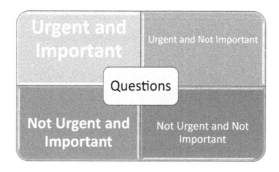

Figure 2.1  Quadrant One Questions (adapted from Steven R. Covey)

that make noise and lots of smoke in order to get their learners' attention. OK, "Hold on!" you say, "I am not going to dress up, entertain, or play stupid games with the learners. Relax . . . I'm not asking you to. Those methods work for those instructors to a certain extent because of their flamboyant characters and extroverted personalities. The adventure of learning is not about watching an instructor. It is about engaging and participating in learning. The problem with flamboyant instructors is that they are doing all the work and hoping the learners will retain something. The real power in learning is that the learners have to be in the driver seat, in the salt mines, exploring the moon, discussing with Darwin, and assisting Madame Curie. Any dedicated instructor can inspire that kind of learning, because it's not about showmanship, it's about asking questions that get to heart of learning: the excitement and enthusiasm generated by acquiring new skills and new understanding.

You may argue, "Learning, i.e. acquiring permanent knowledge and skills, is hard work, usually not fun. Staying clear of the frivolous activities—or 'fun stuff'—prepares learners for college classes, seminars, or workshops that are rigorous, inordinately difficult, and frankly boring." My response is,

> Do you really want them to learn what you are presenting? Do you want them to desire to keep learning when they leave the class? Do you want them to be pleased enough with their learning to want to learn more by enrolling in more college classes, workshops, seminars, or presentations on the subject?

Then make it enjoyable by engaging them mentally, physically, emotionally, and even spiritually.

So, teachers, instructors, professors, trainers . . . **PAY ATTENTION!** If the "learning" in which you want the learners to engage is important (if it is not important, why are you wasting their time and your time?), then you have to make it more noticeable and attention-grabbing than all of the other things vying for the learners' attention. The trick is to give the learners something urgent on which they must focus their attention—like well-formed questions for each learner that invite them to do something.

## 2.7  The Brain Operates at the Speed of Light

We have discussed that the constant competition for our brain's attention poses a large problem for instructors trying to keep learners engaged. Another thing we are dealing with is that the brain operates at a mind-numbing speed (pun intended: it is hard to comprehend how fast our brains really work), approaching the speed of light.[5] When the mind is inactive—or "passive"—what does it do? It doesn't just go into neutral. The mind focuses on something else, day dreams, doodles, or fidgets, for example. Even when we are asleep, we are thinking furiously. Ever heard of the rapid eye movement (REM) cycle? Unless learners are asked to do something, in other words be active in their learning, the brain does not place much of its resources into action. It turns to other things of interest. As mentioned earlier, added to all the sensory distractions, emotions, telephones, music, consumerism, video games, and electronic tune-out tools, instructors have a serious challenge in order to get learners to pay attention.

Youth and adult learners both have to struggle to "pay attention" and actively listen to get the information they need from lectures, endless talking, and whole-class questions. It shouldn't be so hard to learn, but fortunately, the solution is simple: use questions to actively engage the learners. Since the brain works so fast and gets distracted so quickly, pacing is incredibly important in asking questions. When learners are expected to wait for any length of time, that is when even interested and engaged brains begins to wander. Let's face it. Even the most flamboyant and entertaining instructor cannot hold all the learners' attention all the time by themself.

In order to pick up the pace of questioning, the instructor must have a list of questions prepared beforehand and set time limits on answering them (in Chapter 6 you will learn how to write WILD HOG questions before instruction). Popcorn questioning works well in establishing a quick pace and is perfect for small groups of five or six learners. Don't try this with the whole group because it is hard to keep more than six learners on the edge of their seats if they only get asked one question. Assign a participant in each group to be the Question Master and optionally another participant to be the timekeeper. For younger learners, the instructor should be the timekeeper. Each Question Master has a list of five questions that must be answered in a set time, no more than three minutes. The Question Master will rapidly fire the questions at random group members. All the questions will be asked at least three times or until everyone in the group has answered all of them correctly. Incorrectly answered questions are repeated until they get answered correctly. By giving the learners the questions that an instructor would have asked in a whole-group setting and getting them to ask and answer the questions, full engagement is possible. Learners are happy; the instructor is happy, what could be better than that?

In a typical class question–answer session, where one learner at a time answers questions, this provides a perfect opportunity for the "listening" learners' brains to find more interesting things to think about. Another simple fix is to have all the learners answer the question chorally while the instructor roams, checks the answers, and encourages the learners. It is important for the instructor to make the activity more like a game show or competition, rather than an inquisition or drill. The nice thing about this method is that if a participant does not know the answer, as soon as others answer the question, that participant will know the answer. When the instructor asks the question again, that participant will be able to answer on their own. With a list of questions already designed to scaffold and tier the difficulty (WILD HOG), an instructor can rapidly fire questions and keep the pace moving. In the space of 15 minutes, many questions can be asked and answered, and every learner is active and engaged. I must point out again that the instructor must be roaming the classroom and listening as they pass learners answering the questions. If the learner or learners do not provide the correct or appropriate answer, then the instructor needs to backtrack and discover what the misunderstanding or gap in knowledge is (see Section 13.4). When the learning is fast-paced, instructors save time, and because the brain does not get distracted, the content is more likely to sink in to long-term memory.

In this book, when I refer to asking questions, I am always referring to engaging the maximum number of learners for each question. As you were reading through my analysis of learner attitudes regarding instructor questions, you probably thought of several solutions to improve the effectiveness of instruction. In the next chapters, we will explore how to adjust our questions for maximum learning for all learners, not just the ones in front. The entire purpose of this book is to give you the knowledge, tools, and practice to alter the "typical" and largely ineffective questioning traditions and ensure that every learner be given the chance to answer great questions. This book will help you make effective, all-inclusive questioning techniques second nature and will guide you to customizing those questions for the learners for whom you are held accountable. A large part of what I am trying to do in this book is to change the stereotype that the instructor is not effective unless they are in front of the audience, asking questions to the whole group.

## Summary
1  Listening is a passive endeavor that no instructor can control or even monitor. An instructor that engages the learners with something to do changes the participant from passive mode to active mode.
2  Face-to-face learning situations have to deal with the distractions present outside of the learner and within the learner. Synchronous online learning situations have similar distractions with the added distraction of the unseen environment of each remote learner. Asynchronous learning minimizes distractions because each learner must respond to every question or not get credit for attendance and participation.

3   Learners fall into poor learning habits that we allow because of the way that we ask questions. The typical asking questions of one learner at a time does not mean that all learners are learning. It is a large waste of learning time for most learners.

4   Regardless of how good the question is, the manner of asking the question determines how the learner responds to the question.

5   The reticular formation allows us to choose to concentrate and pay attention. In other words, it is the organ responsible for the ability to focus. Each learner receives a torrent of sensory information, only one of which is hearing. Flamboyant teachers shock the learners to get their attention, but the learner is still in passive mode.

6   Urgency is what engages and triggers attention. To aid learners in focusing, the instructor must provide a sense of urgency in order to engage the learners in asking and answering their own questions. Urgency means the actions are time-bound and important. For asynchronous learning, time to answer questions is extended, but the questions must still be important. The quality and genuine nature of the responses are the largest concerns.

7   The brain operates quickly, and any lag causes learners to lose focus. Engaging all of the learners in questioning activities that require fast responses augments learning.

## Questions to Consider

1   How dependent am I on whole-group questions?

_____

_____

2   Recognizing how my learners may respond to whole-group questions will have what effects on my lesson planning?

_____

_____

3   What options do I plan to utilize instead of whole-group questions?

_____

_____

4   What is my current method to get all learners to pay attention?

_____

_____

5   How do I plan to create a sense of urgency in my instruction?

_____

_____

6   How do I plan to implement popcorn questioning in small groups?

_____

_____

7   In what lesson will I employ choral response to popcorn questions?

_____

_____

## Notes

1   Schoolteachers have to remember that, when we are dealing with adolescent minds that are developing and forming, we hope that by the time they get to college they will be independent learners and be resilient enough to withstand the rigors of dry college classes. But, how many of us could say that about our learning experiences? Were we independent learners, thirsty for knowledge and resilient enough to pay attention in long winded lectures? Really, that is the only difference between young learners and adult learners. Young learners won't put up with lessons that don't engage them; they fidget, move around, throw things, or just do something else. We adult learners, on the other hand, have learned to control ourselves, at least outwardly, long enough to not tell the instructor, "Stop talking and let's do something!" Let's face it, while adult learners can plow through the boring stuff, they enjoy participating and being fully engaged just as much as younger learners.

2   There may be an argument that some might be listening actively, but that might be an oxymoronic statement because there is nothing we can do to refine or focus our hearing, and nodding your head and saying "yeah" once in a while is no indication of better hearing.

3   An interesting note about the reticular formation is that it is formed from millions of a special kind of neuron known as interneurons. This type of neuron, rather than having only one long axon that targets only one receiving neuron, has multiple axons that can target multiple receiving and sending neurons (see the drawings of different neurons i.e. bipolar interneuron). http://willistonberg.pbworks.com/w/page/21091185/Shaffer%27s%20Neurology%20Page). The number of possible connections

(synapses) ranges in the trillions. This net (which is what reticular means) of neurons is responsible for managing all of the extremely complex and interconnected muscle commands and associated secondary support systems for those muscles, such as increased nutrients and waste removal (Wang, 2008, p. 205). The reticular formation appears to operate in 90-minute cycles that cause the ability to pay attention to flow and ebb, with the morning time being the most acute and afternoon and evening being the least acute (Sylwester, 1995, pp. 44–45). Is there an instructor that never had to struggle with afternoon classes?

4   For information on the four quadrants described by Steven R. Covey, see https://succeedfeed.com/stephen-covey-4-quadrants-to-be-productive/ Covey, S. (1989). *Seven habits of highly effective people*. New York: Simon & Schuster.

5   (Caine & Caine, 1991, p 80).

## References

Caine, R., & Caine, G. (1991). *Making connections: Teaching and the human brain*. Alexandria, VA: Association for Supervision and Curriculum Development.

Covey, S. (1989). *Seven habits of highly effective people*. New York: Simon & Schuster.

Sylwester, R. (1995). *A celebration of neurons: An educator's guide to the human brain*. Alexandria, VA: Association for Supervision and Curriculum Development.

Wang, D. (2008). Reticular formation and spinal cord injury. *International Spinal Chord Society*, 47(2009), 204–212. https://doi.org/10.1038/sc.2008.105

# 3

# Whole-Brain Questions

## What Types of Questions Are Compatible With Brain-Based Learning?

### 3.1  Power of Questions and the Brain

For over 35 years, researchers have warned us that, without higher-order thinking in the classroom, learners are not effective at recalling or utilizing obtained knowledge.[1] Unfortunately, because the focus of participant learning has been directed toward passing a standardized tests for so long, and schools are routinely punished for low performance, it comes as no surprise that instructors would be tempted to skip the "fun and games" of higher-order thinking and just focus on the minimum standards for all their learners to pass the test. In doing this, however, instructors make the classic error of choosing the short-term benefits at the sacrifice of the long-term results. By not ever getting to dig deeper, learners simply gain the short-term capacity to recall shallow information to pass the test, instead of striving for the long-term benefits of deep, long-term learning. Aside from being fun, engaging, and worthwhile, engaging participants in higher-order thinking, if the lower-order knowledge has been introduced, actually helps push that knowledge and skill into permanent memory. In other words, skipping the cherry on top is not a good idea because it is essential to apply what is learned and get participants thinking about it in order for them to remember it. As Dr. Daniel Willingham[2] affirms, long-term memory (learning) is a result of deep thinking. I think you get the point. If we want to see major strides in participant learning, we cannot afford to continue focusing on minimum standards established by standardized tests.

We have learned that the brain is not composed of isolated right and left hemispheres but that it is a whole system that is employed in all brain functions.[3] Even more important is the research that shows that this whole brain even extends beyond the cranial cavity into the muscles and sensory organs.[4] I keep saying it over and over, "The body is connected to the brain and if you can get the body moving in the right direction, so is the brain." As a result, if we desire to be truly effective at inspiring learning, we must focus more on aligning our "learning promoting actions" (aka teaching) to the way the brain learns best: holistically. This is more than catering to learning preferences identified by common learning styles inventories and more than simply getting their bodies moving. This means that we must ask questions that ask them to do something purposeful to either gain knowledge or apply it.

Our duty as instructors and educators is to incite curiosity, inspire research, and engender deep thinking, all of which create neurological pathways and "habits of mind" that we hope will serve them well in continued study and careers. Our most effective tool is the question, and it has the power to do all of the above and more.

Here are some things that we know about the brain (see Table 3.1).

Table 3.1  Characteristics of the Brain

**What We Know About the Brain (Caine & Caine, 1991)**

| | |
|---|---|
| "The brain is a ***parallel*** processor" <br> *How can we, see, listen, and write at the same time?* | "Learning engages the entire ***physiology***" <br> *Why are skills like riding a bicycle, swimming, or playing an instrument not forgotten?* |
| "The search for ***meaning*** is ***innate***" <br> *Why do we love word puzzles, riddles, and jokes?* | "The search for meaning occurs through '***patterning***'" <br> *Why do the best pieces of music repeat certain melodies and patterns?* |
| "***Emotions*** are critical to patterning" <br> *Why do we remember personal events from childhood so vividly?* | "The brain processes ***parts*** and ***wholes*** simultaneously" <br> *How do we go shopping and not only remember what we need but also keep track of not going over budget?* |
| "Learning involves both ***focused*** attention and ***peripheral*** perception" <br> *How is it that we can learn to dribble a ball and keep track of other players on the court?* | "Learning always involves ***conscious*** and ***unconscious*** processes" <br> *What is it that causes us to remember not only what was written but how we felt when we read it?* |

---

**What We Know About the Brain (Caine & Caine, 1991)**

| | |
|---|---|
| *"We have at least **two** different types of memory: a **spatial** memory system and a set of systems for **rote** learning"* <br> *Why is it that we can remember what we ate for breakfast without effort, but I have to repeat a phone number several times to remember it?* | *"We **understand** and **remember** best when facts and skills are embedded in natural, spatial memory"[5]* <br> *Why is it that we can go to the movies and retell the whole story, plot, main characters, and climax perfectly?* |

---

Questions that match how the brain works provide a way that we can take advantage of the precious little time given us for inspiring learning, and they can help us engage all learners. For example:

Questions that take advantage of the brains' skill at searching for meaning.

> If pro is the opposite of con, what is the opposite of progress?
> Which months of the year have less than 31 days? What would the year be like if each month had 30 days?
> If 5 times B equals 10, what is B?
> How can light be both a wave and a photon?

Questions that search for patterns and meaning.

> What message did Edgar Allen Poe intend when the Raven repeated "Nevermore"?
> When error 504 appears on the computer screen, what is the next step?
> What did the writer mean by stating, ""Chocolate cake is my Achilles heel"?[6]
> The old saying, "Rolling stones gather no moss" could be used in what situations?

Questions that take advantage of your locale or experiential memory.

> Why was the mama bear upset about what Goldilocks had done?
> How did you feel when you first rode a bicycle?
> What other political events were happening in France during the first revolution?
> When you listened to Mozart's Eine Kleine Nachtmusik 1st Movement[7], what stood out to you?
> When you saw the movie "It's a Wonderful Life" by Frank Capra (1946),[8] what did you think about your life?

Questions relating to focused attention.

> When you observed the fish in the bottle, what did you see that was unusual?
> How can you correct the process and arrive at the right answer?
> After reading your essay again, what elements can you improve?
> When listening to an irate customer, what should you be thinking?
> When diagnosing a computer problem, what steps should you take first?

I've already mentioned that the body is connected to the brain[9] and that by using multiple sensory organs in the learning an instructor can raise the chances of long-term memory dramatically.[10] I had the opportunity to be the executive director over a small elementary charter school that used this principle to great effect. Since charters each have their own specialty (or gimmick) to attract parents to enroll their learners, this one was no different. They built their instructional platform on a system of learning created by a German educator known as Rudolf Stiener.[11] His philosophy was that you have to instruct the whole child, not just their brains. Included in his curriculum were heavy doses of art, movement, music, and drama. As a tribute to the effectiveness of this philosophy, graduates of the Waldorf curricula have become well-known artists and professionals.[12] My point in bringing this up is that to increase memory (learning), increase the number of ways the human body can interact with knowledge or skills. We can easily ask questions and request answers that require the body to become involved as in art, music, movement, or creation (building, problem-solving, STEM etc.).

## Questions Answered by Creating

> How could you represent the interaction of an acid with a base in a song?
> What would the answer to this math problem look like if you drew a picture of it?
> What kind of movements could you create that would allow you to express logical operations without words?
> How could you devise a dance that would indicate the act of chemical covalent bonding?
> How could you turn the war of 1812 into a drama?
> If you had only straws to build with, how would you build a suspension bridge?
> If you put music to the Rhyme of the Ancient Mariner, what would it sound like?
> If you transformed the algebraic Postulates and Axioms into magical rules, what kind of spells would you use with your wand to perform algebra?

How would you explain the fall of the Romans in an exciting story?

If you could paint pictures of before and after "D" day, what would s look like?

If you were teaching six-year-old children about the life cycle of a butterfly, how would you do it?

## 3.2 HOTS and Questions

### How Can Questions Lead to Brain-Based, Higher-Order Thinking?

Before we dive into brain-based learning, I need to clarify some terminology—or, better stated, buzzwords, overused nomenclature, or even cliches about thinking. Without thinking about what we are saying (grin), we often lump the different types of thinking into the category of "thinking harder" when we indiscriminately interchange the terms "critical thinking" with "problem solving" and "analytical thinking." When I use these terms, it will be to identify a particular type of thinking that requires unique cognitive functions that are designed to produce specific results. It stands to reason, therefore, that to incite your learners to engage in analytical thinking a question must be posed that requires analytical thinking in order to answer it (see Section 8.2).

As discussed in Chapter 6, the skill and the art of teaching is to get each learner to engage their brain on the question. Assume that the delivery of the question is effective, and the learner is confronted with the question. Thinking begins, but the type of thinking as referred to earlier depends on the question. Speaking of the brain, we know there are two types of learning systems. Taxon memory is behavioristic and depends on repeated stimulus and response, like the repetition you need to remember a phone number. Locale memory is experiential, which means that instant memories are created because of an experience like watching a movie or observing a momentous occasion.[13] In the lower levels of Bloom's Taxonomy that we will discuss later, knowledge, facts, and data are pushed from short-term memory to long-term memory through consistent repetition. In the higher levels of Bloom's Taxonomy, locale memory is used because of the nature of the learning at those levels lends itself to experiences such as: experiments, discovery, exploration, creation, group work, design learning, project-based learning, etc. Because these experiences create instantaneous memories, learning is more enjoyable and more effective. Locale memory learning activities, used after Taxon memory learning activities, cause learners to think deeply, and as one of my favorite authors Dr. Daniel Willingham says, "Memory is the residue of thought."[14] When learners think deeply, they not only learn facts and topics but understand concepts, generalizations, principles, and theories that can be transferred to other knowledge, concepts, principles, and theories.[15] In short, using locale memory systems that engage learners in deep thinking makes learning (memory) permanent. Isn't that what we want? Unfortunately, these higher-level learning experiences are often skipped as unessential or, even worse, too much work for the instructor to prepare. This backward thinking, however, is like preparing a sandwich without the meat, leaving learners unsatisfied with their educational experience and asking "Where's the beef?"

Certainly, we want our learners to "think harder." More specifically, we want them to take the knowledge that they have gained and be able to do something with it. This process of being able to do something with acquired knowledge and skills takes consistent review and effort. First, concrete foundations of knowledge need to be created in a learner's mind before they will be able to use them as a platform for leaping into the unknown. Stated more simply, the beginning step of learning is acquiring knowledge and obtaining understanding (using taxon memory). Once that is accomplished, then the higher-order thinking must be engaged to permanently fix that knowledge into the learner's brain (using locale memory).

Volumes have already been said about higher-order thinking skills (HOTS), but there may be someone reading this book who may appreciate a minor review.[16] Here's the quick review: Dr. Benjamin S. Bloom (1956), in mapping the cognitive domain (he mapped other domains, but nobody remembers them), explained that some mental activities are harder to do than others. He created a hierarchy we call "Bloom's Taxonomy": Knowledge, Comprehension, Application, Analysis, Synthesis, and Evaluation (see Figure 3.1). The general consensus is that Dr. Bloom and his team had it mostly right, but that synthesis and evaluation should be switched. I am in agreement

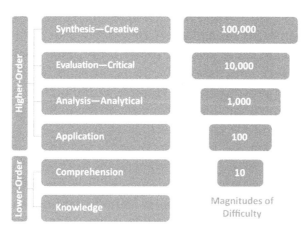

**Figure 3.1** Dr. Benjamin Bloom's Chart of Cognitive Difficulty

with this conclusion because I believe that it is more difficult to create things than to criticize things. Bloom's Taxonomy has been refined, reworked, and discussed ad nauseum in education circles, but amazingly, the foundational principles are irrefutable and apparently timeless. HOTS are described as the "application level and above" skills.

As educators, we still talk a lot about striving to get the learners to the higher levels, but in reality, we teach mainly in the lower levels. Starting with that is necessary because learners cannot tackle the "application and above" mental functions until they have acquired knowledge and understanding, the concrete foundation. The tragedy that exists in many classrooms is that, because of a need to get through the material, or the constant pressure to make sure the minimums are acquired, or—in the case of public schools—to prepare learners for the state exams, often educators, instructors, and trainers never get to the HOTS level in their instruction. The failure to reach the higher stratosphere of thinking brings about two major consequences: 1) learners amass great amounts of knowledge but have little ability to make it useful and 2) learners begin to acquaint learning with unpleasant drudgery (constant memorization using only taxon memory).

Don't get me wrong. Real, honest-to-goodness learning takes considerable effort and discipline, but there is no rule stating that the learning process must be unenjoyable. Another systemic reason for not getting to the HOTS is that of convenience for the instructor. It is so much easier just to tell the learner the answer rather than to create a learning situation in which the learner will discover the answer themselves. One point I would like to make is this—and please highlight this—while it takes more work and preparation and ultimately trust for the instructor to prepare HOTS learning, the benefits, in my opinion, outweigh any inconvenience.

What are the benefits for the learners to engage in HOTS learning? The first is that thinking experiences pushes the knowledge and skills into long-term memory, and the second is that it is much more enjoyable to apply, analyze, criticize, and create than it is to memorize and practice. The bottom line is that learners exposed to HOTS questions become more efficient and effective learners, meaning they remember the content better and longer because of the locale memory system capacity to create instant long-term memories. More importantly for instructors and long-term learning, if learners are prepared for higher-order thinking, they are more interested (engaged and not causing disruptions) in what they are doing because the learners are the decision makers on how they will answer the questions the instructors pose to them, and, because of the good learning experiences, the learners will be open for additional learning (we all have our classroom horror stories and use them frequently to justify our aversion and ineptitude in math, science, history, etc.).

"Nobody succeeds beyond their wildest expectations unless they begin with some wild expectations." Ralph Charell was right when he stated those words in his book *How to Make Things Go Your Way*. Learners will never reach genius level unless instructors challenge them with genius-level questions to answer. Instructors have to use effective questions to "prime the pump" of learner thinking, and, once the learners get going, they must feed them more genius-level questions. Dr. Daniel Willingham (2010), a cognitive scientist and author of *Why Don't Students Like School?*, cautions that if the questions are too hard, learners will not answer them, and if they are too easy, they will ignore them.[17] The ability to tackle hard questions has to be developed and nurtured over time; it doesn't happen all at once. In my book *Teaching Students to Dig Deeper* I discuss that one of the qualities of a college-/career-ready learner is the ability to deal with questions and problems that force the learners to venture into the unfamiliar.[18]

Brain-based questions that push learners to use HOTS have predictable structures (see Table 3.2). First off, they are open-ended questions that require

Table 3.2

---

**Examples of HOTS Questions**

---

| HOTS | Characteristic | Question |
|---|---|---|
| Application | Explain | How do you use fractions to bake a cake? |
| Application | Apply | What do you do when someone cuts their finger severely? |
| Application | Design | How would you design an economy using Adam Smith's economic philosophy? |
| Application | Extend | If I create an email, what do I need to do to send it to multiple people? |
| Analysis | Categorize | How would you categorize the contents of your backpack or purse? |
| Analysis | Compare | What is unique about the characteristics of water? |
| Analysis | Process | What steps would you take to convince someone to buy your product? |
| Analysis | Contrast | What challenges that Abraham Lincoln faced do not apply today? |
| Evaluation | Choose | If the cars cost the same, how will you choose which one to buy? |

## Examples of HOTS Questions

| HOTS | Characteristic | Question |
|---|---|---|
| Evaluation | Opine | What did you think about the plot of Macbeth? Why? |
| Evaluation | Criticize | What suggestions for improvement would you give the customer service representative? |
| Evaluation | Distinguish | Which colors coincide best when composing a piece of art? |
| Synthesis | Construct | If I gave you 12 straws and 11 marshmallows, what could you build? |
| Synthesis | Hypothesize | What lasting effects of the end of World War II do we see today? |
| Synthesis | Create | In *Study in Scarlet*[19] from Sherlock Holmes, how would you have ended the story? |
| Synthesis | Predict | Given the two bar graphs showing growth of two investments, how would you invest $10,000? |

a sentence or a paragraph to answer. They are impossible to answer with yes or no or one or two words. The next characteristic is that these questions tend to be divergent, not convergent. What I mean by that is that divergent questions have multiple right answers and open up more questions, rather than leading to one single correct answer. Another characteristic of HOTS questions is that they give the learners a certain amount of liberty on how to answer them. Finally, HOTS-friendly questions often require logic, deduction, and supposition.

## Summary
1   Using questions that promote higher-order thinking should not be considered optional because it actually increases memory (learning).
2   The brain has particular skills and abilities that are often overlooked in the business of instruction and learning.
3   Aligning our questions to better fit the way our learners think makes learning easier and more effective.
4   The body is connected to the brain. If the body is engaged in learning activities, like creation, then so is the brain.
5   Dr. Benjamin Bloom created a taxonomy of six mental activities, each a magnitude more difficult than the prior: Knowledge, Comprehension, Application, Analysis, Evaluation, and Synthesis. The last four activities are referred to as the higher-order thinking skills (HOTS).

6    Because of the pressure to cover the required material for passing the test and the fact that preparing HOTS learning activities requires extra effort, many instructors rarely engage their learners with HOTS questions.

7    HOTS questions not only improve memory but provide a more pleasant learning experience.

8    In order to ask HOTS questions, the groundwork of knowledge and comprehension should be in place.

9    HOTS questions are open-ended, divergent, and permit the answer to come in many forms.

## Questions to Consider

1    How aligned to the brain are my questions?

_____

_____

_____

2    In my current instruction, what brain-aligned questions could I write?
   a    Questions that take advantage of the brains' skill at searching for meaning.

_____

_____

_____

   b    Questions that search for patterns and meaning.

_____

_____

_____

   c    Questions that take advantage of your locale or experiential memory.

_____

_____

_____

   d    Questions relating to focused attention.

_____

_____

_____

3   In my current instruction, what questions could I create that would pro-
    mote creation through art, music, dance, STEM, etc.?

_____

_____

_____

_____

_____

_____

_____

_____

4   In the current topic of study, what questions could I create that use HOTS?
    a   Questions for Application (Implement, Follow, Apply, Process, Oper-
        ate, Do, Calculate, Tabulate, Record).

_____

_____

    b   Questions for Analysis (Compare, Contrast, Categorize, Organize,
        Observe).

_____

_____

    c   Questions for Evaluation (Decide, Choose, Pick, Rank, Prioritize,
        Evaluate, Grade, Rate, Criticize).

_____

_____

    d   Questions for Synthesis (Combine, Create, Design, Build, Plan, Pre-
        dict, Postulate, Solve, Fix, Resolve).

_____

_____

_____

## Notes

1 (Sahin & Kulm, 2008, p. 222)
2 "Memory is the residue of thought," a powerful quote that I will repeat often, from Dr. Daniel Willingham's book, *Why Students Don't Like School*."
3 (Caine & Caine, 1991, p. 34).
4 (Wang, 2008).
5 (Taken from Caine & Caine, 1991).
6 Allusions are something that a well-read or literate person can make sense of. Here are some other examples https://blog.prepscholar.com/allusion-examples.
7 Familiar music of *Mozart Eine Kleine Nachtmusik 1st Movement*, performed here by a quartet in a concert in C. D. Deshmukh Auditorium, India International Centre, Delhi 2014: https://youtu.be/cQuE4otVycQ. You will recognize this music because it is used in many movies: www.allegro-c.de/formate/cmm.htm, Ace Ventura, Charlie's Angels, and many others.
8 I love *It's a Wonderful Life*, but I'm a sap and cry every time. www.imdb.com/title/tt0038650/
9 I visited an aquarium and came to the exhibit where the octopi were held. On the wall of the aquarium was a small sign that told something about the creatures. It stated, "An octopus' brain extends to its limbs." It did not explain more, but it made me think. Does that mean that a physical part of the brain exists outside of the cranial cavity? Or does that mean that parts of the nervous system of octopi can carry on thinking functions? Upon further reflection, What does that mean to humans? Our sensory and motor functions are connected to our brains. What effect do they have on thinking and memory? Is there such a thing as muscle mathematics memory?
10 For a good example of this, take a look at section 13.2 of an instructor's experience with a photosynthesis lesson.
11 In the 1920s, Rudolf Steiner was asked to create the ideal school for a German tobacco company's workers. He called the school Waldorf—yes it is related to the Waldorf Astoria hotels, because the same person owned both. The foundation for the school was that the child's learning should match their developmental growth to maturity. As a result, the Waldorf curriculum of today seeks to do the same thing by engaging the student's head, heart, and hands through art, movement, song, literature, and spiritual development (anthroposophy). For more information on the Waldorf

philosophy and schools, see www.waldorfeducation.org/ or https://ecswe.eu/

12  For more information on Waldorf schools, here is a compendium of their famous graduates: www.thewaldorfs.waldorf.net/

13  Caine and Caine (1991).

14  This is one of the gems of Daniel Willingham's book, *Why Don't Students Like School?*, now in its second edition.

15  See the discussion Lynn Erickson's work on Conceptual Understanding at https://us.corwin.com/sites/default/files/upm-binaries/82739_Chapter_1___Tools_for_Teaching_Conceptual_Understanding%2C_Secondary.pdf

16  Here is a great comparison of the old and the revised Bloom's Taxonomy from Old Dominion University by Overbaugh and Shultz https://web.archive.org/web/20130119235736/http://ww2.odu.edu/educ/rover-bau/Bloom/blooms_taxonomy.htm)

17  Dr. Daniel Willingham wrote a book called *Why Don't Students Like School?*, and he discusses the idea that, although we can increase our capacity to think, and we like doing it as long as it is not too difficult, thinking is not our brain's greatest strength. He maintains that we compensate for this by avoiding thinking and relying on memory, hence the large storage capacity of the cerebral cortex. For a synopsis of his articles, see (http://chem-review.net/blog/?p=321) (10—Willingham's Columns: Cognitive Science for Educators retrieve 11/3/2020

18  One of the ten college- and career- readiness attributes that I discovered was flexibility (i.e. they are able and willing to cope with frustration and ambiguity). My book is found at www.routledge.com/Teaching-Students-to-Dig-Deeper-Ten-Essential-Skills-for-College-and-Career/Johnson/p/book/9781138055858/

19  If you would like to read this, here it is: https://sherlock-holm.es/stories/pdf/a4/1-sided/stud.pdf. How would you have ended the story?

## References

Bloom, B. S. (1956). *Taxonomy of educational objectives, handbook I: The cognitive domain*. New York: David McKay Co Inc.

Caine, R., & Caine, G. (1991). *Making connections: Teaching and the human brain*. Alexandria, VA: Association for Supervision and Curriculum Development.

Capra, F. (1946). *It's a wonderful life*. Liberty Films, Paramount Pictures. Retrieved from www.imdb.com/title/tt0038650/

Sahin, A., & Kulm, G. (2008). Sixth grade mathematics teachers' intension and use of probing, guiding, and factual questions. *Journal of Math Teacher Education, 2008*(11), 221–241. https://doi.org/10.1007/s10857-008-9071-2

Wang, D. (2008). Reticular formation and spinal cord injury. *International Spinal Chord Society, 47*(2009), 204–212. https://doi.org/10.1038/sc.2008.105

Willingham, D. (2010). *Why don't students like school?* San Francisco, CA: Jossey-Bass.

# 4

# Virtual Questioning Distinctions

## How Does That Differ From In-Person Questions?

Morgan-Thomas and Dudau (2019) performed an interesting study on learner engagement online. They discovered that there were three types of online learners, whom they labeled hogs, opossums, and horses in their analysis. The hog-type learners were voracious and indiscriminate in how they participated in online discussions, quizzes, and chats. They did everything. The opossums were discriminate online feeders and participated to a moderate extent, while the horses refused to participate voluntarily. The researchers wanted to know what affected engagement more: pedagogy or content. They proposed that the opossums would be the ideal online learners because they participated selectively in learning resources that benefitted their personal learning goals.[1] I propose that the creation of effective online questions will have the capacity to reach all three types of online learners. Whether you are involved with synchronous or asynchronous online learning, here are some things to consider when crafting questions for your online learners to answer. Synchronous online learning poses some challenges that can be mitigated to some extent, and it also has opportunities.

## 4.1 Setting Expectations

When asking questions to an online classroom, if the instructor has not set the expectation that all learners show actual video of themselves, then there is the temptation for learners to simply log in and then do something else or multitask and only partially listen. In this scenario, the instructor can miss out on visual and facial cues that would indicate a reaction to what is being presented. This is one of the advantages of synchronous online learning. The instructor can see all of the learners' faces without having to wander the room or lose focus on some while paying attention to others. The entire class fits on one screen, and the instructor can easily flag learners who may have questions or something to contribute but who have not for one reason or another. In order for this to work, the instructor must already have warned the learners that they may be given the opportunity to share at any time. Make sure the learners know about muting and unmuting their microphones at appropriate times. In synchronous learning, individuals can speak, and so can small groups, but having all the microphones on at the same time is counterproductive.

Some might view synchronous online learning as limiting how they teach. If we allow it to do so, it will, with a vengeance. An uncareful instructor will become a talking head, and few if any learners will engage. A savvy, tech-proficient instructor, like yourself, will structure the learning in a way that will enhance learning beyond what could be done in the face-to-face classroom. Here are some ideas that excellent asynchronous instructors already use to great advantage.

## 4.2 High-Tech and Low-Tech Solutions

There are high-tech and low-tech solutions to every online classroom learning need. If you are blessed to have the technology and software such as a robust online learning management system (LMS), then you can create learning partners, triads, four square groups, content caucuses, or debate forums in which learners will answer and ask questions that you have designed and prepared them to answer and ask. You can assure that learners are not only active but engaged as you visit these different chat rooms, conversation spaces, or forums. Knowing human nature, your visits have to be more than just a pulse check, asking them to respond every few minutes.

For low-tech situations, email is wonderful, just require that they cc you on all of their conversations and continue their conversation on the same threads (subject line of the email) that you assign them. If they change the subject line of the email, it starts a new thread and causes more work for everyone. In high-tech or low-tech situations, the job of the instructor is to set up the structure of learning, the expectations, and the content, including questions, and then the online instructor becomes the quality control manager, commenting, encouraging, and calling out successes publicly and errors privately. In Chapter 5 we will visit the concept of substantive engagement,

**Table 4.1** Motivational Response Progression in Asynchronous Learning

| *List of Common Comments for Learner Feedback* |
| --- |
| *You accurately responded and appropriately supported your response with evidence and the citation of where you obtained the evidence. Well done! What other ideas might occur to you that would enhance your answer?* |
| *Excellent response! I appreciate the attention to detail in answering the complete questions. You also documented your evidence with correct citations. What do you think about . . . ?* |
| *You obviously put some thought into your answer. Thank you. Please also include evidence supporting your thoughts and the citation of where you found the evidence. Where might you find more information to support your ideas?* |
| *Thank you for your effort. I believe that you are getting close. Please also consider this point . . . or that point . . . and resubmit your answer, including evidence and citations.* |
| *Thank for answering this question. Your answer indicates that you misunderstood the question. Maybe this will help . . . (restate the question in different words). Please resubmit with evidence and citations.* |
| *Please respond in a substantive fashion, not just your opinion. This includes answering the questions completely and providing evidence from research or the texts with appropriate citations. Please resubmit.* |
| *Please get in touch with me through. . . . I'd like to chat with you about your answer.* |

but for now, the instructor must check and let the learners know that they are checking by making comments, suggestions, and critiques in the chat rooms or emails. If you are thinking that this takes dedication, time, and energy, you are correct. It is easy to be a talking head and let participants learn if they want to or not. One thing that helped me to be more interactive is to have a Word document with the most common responses already prepared (see Table 4.1). This allowed me to provide comments to everyone but let me focus on the learners that needed personal attention. Remember that in either synchronous or asynchronous learning (and in person), the goal is to get every learner to answer questions.

## 4.3 Preparing Online Questions

Now that we've looked at the format of online learning, let's get down to preparing questions. The key to successful online questions is anticipating learner responses and reactions. In face-to-face or synchronous online learning scenarios, effective instructors use a series of questions that correspond to learner responses. Asynchronous online instructors can do the same thing, only there is a lag between the question and the time the answer arrives. One simple trick to save your time and the learner's is to combine more than one question, two or three at most. Asynchronous learners are able to find answers and be thoughtful in their responses, so multiple questions or complex questions are no problem.

## Focus the Questions

Just as in face-to-face learning, the more focused your questions are the more efficient and effective they will be. So, let's start with the purpose of asking the question. On the surface it may appear that the purpose of asking a question is obvious; we want the learner to answer the question. Yes, we do want the learner to answer the question, but if we do not clarify that assumption, then all of our questions will be recall and low-level questions. Perhaps a better way to say "purpose" is to identify what type of "thinking" you want the learner to perform in order to answer the question. As we learned earlier, thinking skills range from moderately easy to extremely difficult, recall being on the easy end of the spectrum. In face-to-face learning, the first questions should be easy, then progress to more difficult, i.e. cognitively challenging questions. I propose that, in asynchronous online learning, starting with knowledge-based questions is unnecessary. In order to answer a cognitively challenging question correctly, the base knowledge is assumed. If the learner reads or hears the recorded question and doesn't know the basics, the learner can go back through the notes, lectures, videos, and readings and find the base information in order to answer the question. This is not a bad thing. In fact, it helps the learner do two things. In the process of looking for base information, the learner answers his own question, "What is the endoplasmic reticulum?" When the learner is asking the questions, then the learner is more apt to remember the answer. The second thing that this process does is illustrate to the learner that it is easier to learn as you go, rather than having to backtrack all the time, saving time and energy.

## Provide Clear Instructions

In order to make the responses easy to evaluate, it helps to provide clarity in the question. "In no more than 20 words, in complete sentences, describe a rhombus to a blind man." If you do not provide clarification and tell the learners what you are expecting them to do, then don't be surprised if they give you the minimum one-word answer. It helps to draft your own ideal answer to the question and then include, explicitly, the non-negotiable elements that you require. Whether that be to give examples, provide evidence, include graphs or visuals, cite sources, or use correct spelling, you decide. In Section 3.2 we discussed rigor in terms of the complexity of the question and the difficulty of the thinking skills required to understand the question and to answer the question.

## Summary

1   Just as in face-to-face learning, online instructors need to set the expectations of what online learning is supposed to look like for their class. This includes how to respond to questions and, for synchronous learning, making sure the video is turned on and the microphone muted.
2   Just because it is online learning does not mean that learners cannot effectively collaborate in pairs, small groups, and other configurations.
3   If the synchronous online instructor does not build in interaction with the learners, then he becomes a talking head, easy to disregard and ignore. Synchronous learning is similar to face-to-face in that questions can be asked to groups of learners and individual learners. Questions should be tiered from knowledge and comprehension to HOTS.
4   When monitoring responses, it helps to have a list of common responses prepared to allow you to give attention to more learners.
5   Asynchronous learning can start with the HOTS questions because the learners have time to look up answers and prepare good responses.
6   When writing questions for online learning—and for face-to-face learning—the clearer and more specific the questions are, the better the answers will be.

## Questions to Consider

1   Knowing about learner perceptions—and as a learner yourself—how will you adjust your questioning to anticipate and eliminate negative perceptions and attitudes?

_____

_____

_____

2   What methods will you employ to get your learners' attention?

_____

_____

_____

3 How do you plan to implement a sense of urgency in your face-to-face or online learning?

_____

_____

_____

4 What are your plans to take advantage of the speed of the brain in your questioning?

_____

_____

_____

5 In online learning, what expectations will you communicate to your learners about how to participate in answering questions?

_____

_____

_____

6 In synchronous learning, what is your plan to engage every participant with questions?

_____

_____

_____

7 In asynchronous learning, what is your plan to use questions to engage every participant?

_____

_____

_____

## Note

1 This is an intriguing study about online engagement. Their situation was a graduate course and the online portion was voluntary. If you want to read it, here is the abstract and for a price you can read the whole thing: https://journals.aom.org/doi/abs/10.5465/amle.2018.0029

# Reference

Morgan-Thomas, A., & Dudau, A. (2019). Of possums, hogs, and horses: Capturing the duality of student engagement in eLearning. *Academy of Management Learning & Education*, *18*(4), 564–580. https://doi.org/10.5465/amle.2018.0029v

# 5

## Substantiveness

### How Can Questions Promote Deep Thinking?

Substantive questions are heavy-duty, something to sink your teeth into. It means that when you ask a substantive question, you show that you have done your research, you connect it with other knowledge, and you request thoughtful answers that do the same thing. Substantiveness is the gold standard for responses to questions. If a learner does not provide a sufficiently thought-out answer, or if the answer is incomplete, or if the answer is incorrect, good instructors will not let the learner remain in error. A good instructor will ask follow-up questions, probe for more information, and ask leading questions to help the learner arrive at a more acceptable response. Substantiveness is not a natural state for learners to adopt.[1] More often than not, learners would much rather answer superficial responses that require little thinking and less knowledge.

### 5.1 Model Learner Expectations

If we want our learners to be accurate and independent thinkers, then slideshows, presentations, and any materials that we put in their hands to study must have appropriate citations as a model for them to follow. It doesn't matter what citation method is used, whether it is MLA, Chicago, or APA, just be consistent (I prefer APA). When I did my doctoral studies, mostly online asynchronously, my professors expected any comment that we made to supported by outside evidence and a citation from the texts or other research. As a result, quoting text or summarizing and then adding the citations became second nature to me. It was then that I realized that somehow K–12 education got a pass on citing information and works from other authors in their presentations and materials. Most university professors are consistent about citing work, but business presentations and materials are in the same boat as public education—very few citations. Where ever plagiarism is found, it should be avoided like the plague.

Your learners deserve to know the source from which you are getting your information. Academic honesty and primarily the avoidance of plagiarism demands that when the thought, idea, data, or words come from another person or group, they must be recognized. It is no wonder that business professionals, journalists, college students, and even teachers have little qualms about borrowing other's work, because, since they began going to school, the only time they saw citations was in high school or college when they had to write their term papers. If the textbooks do not use citations and their instructors do not use citations, how is citing the evidence supposed to become second nature? The instructors, presenters, trainers, and professors need to cite their sources and model what they want their learners to do.

## Model Evidence

While we may often have great ideas, thoughts, and words, we must understand the importance of providing evidence to strengthen and bolster our stance. When asking questions verbally, acknowledge the source in the question.

"As written by Poe, 'The Raven' may represent the finality of life. What clues has he provided that would support that opinion?"

But questions in written form should also include when Poe wrote 'The Raven' and in what publication.[2]

"In the poem, 'The Raven' Poe represents the finality of life. What clues has he provided that would support that opinion? Please answer in at least 100 words and support your opinion quoting the line from the poem that corresponds."

Poe, E. (1845). *The Raven*. New York: The New York Mirror.

Poe, E. (1845). *The Raven*. Retrieved December 21, 2020, from http://theravenpoe.com/

## 5.2 Set Clear Expectations for Responses

Speaking of logic, if imprecise or vague questions promote imprecise and vague answers, if any at all given that the learners might not understand the questions, then the more clear and straightforward the question is, the more clear and straightforward the answers will be. For example, "What does this mean?" or "Why is that?" would be much better as "What does Edgar Allen Poe mean when he wrote, 'Nameless here for evermore,' in the poem the Raven?" or "Why does the color of the liquid in the flask turn purple when you add a boiled cabbage solution?"

For face-to-face or synchronous learning, learners need to be informed on the manner in which you desire them to answer the questions. Answering questions effectively does not happen naturally. As instructors, we have to train them to do it and then consistently practice it with them. At the very least, all learners, even elementary-school children, need to answer the questions in full sentences. Often it helps to provide a sentence stem to help the learners complete their thoughts appropriately. Older learners should be trained to take part of the question and place it at the beginning of their response.

> Question: "How do you tell the age of a tree or how do you tell the age of a turtle?"
> Answer: "You tell the age of a tree by counting the rings in a cross section of the trunk. You estimate the age of a turtle by counting the rings in the plates on their shell called scutes and then divide by two.[3]"

For virtual asynchronous learning and written questions, it is essential that the instructor indicate what length of response would be appropriate. If no parameters are given, the "hog"-type learners, as discussed earlier in Chapter 4, may write a 1,000 word thesis, while the "horse"-type learner will only write three words. The format is simply: *the question* followed by the *instructions for the answer*, the *length in words*, and then the *reference for the question*.

Example:

"How did the Battle of Hastings help the Normans become the rulers of England? Answer in complete sentences and provide evidence of your opinion. Always cite from where you got this information."

## 5.3 Model Logic and Reasoning

I was always confused about who was implying and who was inferring. Syllogisms, deduction, induction, abduction, and Boolean searches are all confusing, since most people do not know what they are other than the application of logic. In fact, we do them a disservice if we simply lump them all together as "deduction," because each requires a different kind of thinking or, perhaps, a different perspective of thinking.

In making questions more complex, logic and all its forms previously mentioned depend on small words, or in mathematics we could call them operators.[4] These operators, when used in questions, have the power to raise the thinking required to answer the question and cause the question to be more complex and therefore enhance the rigor of the question. Erickson's Concept-Based Curriculum (Erickson, Lanning, & French, 2017) also relates complexity of thinking with different types of knowledge.[5] We use these logical operators in communication all the time. The word "and" is conjunctive, meaning it takes two or more items and joins their meaning. The same also can be said for "but, although, nevertheless, however, yet etc." For example, for "and/not" there are conjunctive questions and disjunctive questions and for "or" there are inclusive and exclusive questions (see Table 5.1).

**Table 5.1** Increasing Substantiveness Using Logic

| *Logical Questions to Raise Substantiveness* | |
| --- | --- |
| *Conjunctive Questions (And, but, although, yet, nevertheless, etc.)* | • How does water expand when it freezes, and what effect does that peculiar trait have on the world?<br>• What happens when you add hydrogen to chlorine, and what reagent do you need?<br>• How was Troy destroyed and why?<br>• Why does it rain in Spain but never on the plain?<br>• What did Winston Churchill accomplish as a great statesman yet fail to accomplish as Prime Minister?[6] |
| *Disjunctive Exclusive Or Questions (XOR) (One or the other but not both)* | • Which would you rather do, pet a snake or tickle an alligator?<br>• Should I correct my spelling now, or should I work on my grammar?<br>• Why does a dragon have scales, or why does a dragon not have scales? |
| *Disjunctive Inclusive Or Questions (One, the other, or both)* | • How do you solve the addition problem, or how do you solve the multiplication problem?<br>• What is the best job in the world, or how much money do you want to make?<br>• How did the exponent change the graph, or what was the result of the equation? |
| *Negation Questions* | • Why aren't polar bears brown?<br>• How is it false that erosion is caused by the sun?<br>• What if the earth was not the planet third-closest to the sun? |

## Summary

1   Substantive means the answer to the question must be well thought-out, on target, and supported by evidence. The first step in establishing a substantive answer is modeling correct citation of sources.

2   In order to get good substantive answers, the questions themselves must be well prepared and documented. The learners need to know how to answer questions substantively, and this requires training on what expectations the instructor has. In written questions, these kinds of details can be included in the question.

3   Substantive questions—or questions with meat in them—can be derived from reasoning skills such as the use of logical operators: and, or, and not.

## Questions to Consider

1   In your current instruction, how could you increase the substantiveness of your questions?

_____

2   Write three substantive questions (including citing sources).

_____

_____

_____

3   What level of substantiveness are the answers you typically receive from your questions?

_____

4   What could you do to improve the expectations for substantiveness either for oral answers or answers in writing?

_____

5   Jot down the length, detail, and level of evidence you would like your learners to provide.

_____

6   Write a conjunctive question in your current area of study.

_____

_____

7   Write an inclusive disjunctive question in your current area of study.

_____

_____

8   Write an exclusive disjunctive question in your current area of study.

_____

_____

9   Write a negation question in your current area of study.

_____

_____

## Notes

1   In fact, in this study about learners categorized as hogs, opossums, and horses, they surmise that just because a learner answers questions and participates behaviorally does not mean that cognitively they are engaged: MORGAN-THOMAS, A., & DUDAU, A. (2019). Of Possums, Hogs, and Horses: Capturing the Duality of Student Engagement in Elearning. *Academy of Management Learning & Education*, 18(4), 564–580. https://doi.org/10.5465/amle.2018.0029

2   It also helps if you provide a url link that allows the learner to see for themselves. http://theravenpoe.com/. If you wish to read all of Poe's works, Project Gutenburg has them here for free: www.gutenberg.org/ebooks/search/?query=edgar+allan+poe

3   It is only an estimate, because the rings are periods of growth not directly related to season, though in winter it can be assumed that less growth occurs because of hibernation or scarcity: www.petmd.com/reptile/care/how-tell-turtles-age

4   This site provides a detailed explanation of logical operators: https://philosophy.lander.edu/logic/conjunct.html

5   H. Lyn Erickson is the "godmother" of concept-based curriculum. The idea that concept knowledge transfers but not factual knowledge is foundational to her theories. If learners understand one concept, they can transfer that knowledge or generalize it to other situations. Erickson, H. Lynn, Lanning, Lois A. and French, Rachel. (2017). Concept-Based

Curriculum and Instruction for the Thinking Classroom Second Edition. Corwin a SAGE Publishing Company. ISBN 9781506355399.

6    Winston Churchill was famous in the war and well celebrated in his international politics, but he lost the election of 1945 right after the war because he ignored the economic conditions in England, giving the labor party opportunity to convince the people that socialism was the way to go. https://winstonchurchill.hillsdale.edu/election-loss-1945/

## References

Morgan-Thomas, A., & Dudau, A. (2019). Of possums, hogs, and horses: Capturing the duality of student engagement in eLearning. *Academy of Management Learning & Education*, 18(4), 564–580. https://doi.org/10.5465/amle.2018.0029

Erickson, H. L., Lanning, L. A., & French, R. (2017). *Concept-based curriculum and instruction for the thinking classroom* (2nd ed.). Corwin a SAGE Publishing Company. ISBN 9781506355399

# Section I

## Questioning Foundation Conclusion

Why do you ask questions?

You have to be able to answer that question, because your answer will be the determining factor in establishing the effectiveness of all the questions you ask. Of the four common reasons for asking questions discussed in Chapter 1, which is the most important and which is the least important: Assessment, Motivation, Thinking, or Teaching? Your priorities will govern how you organize your lessons. Knowing how the participants in your learning view typical questions and having a better idea of how the brain works will also help you to design questions that get to the heart of what you as an instructor are trying to do: inspire learning. Recognizing that there are differences in virtual and face-to-face learning will help you anticipate and adjust for using questions effectively. Finally, setting the standard for substantive answers begins with creating substantive questions.

In every organization there is an evaluation process, and in each, especially for K–12 educators, there is a portion of the evaluation that rates your personal improvement goals. A specific plan to improve specific questioning skills is a perfect fit for such yearly evaluations. Take a few minutes and jot down some things that you would like to improve in your questioning for each chapter of this section under the activity column. For example, you may want to know more about how the brain works. Then list what resources you will need. You might want to attend more training or read a book about the brain and learning. Then establish a day that you plan to get this done. Don't forget to look at the end notes for each chapter for additional sources of learning that you may want to include in your plan.

Section I  Questioning Foundation Professional Growth Plan

| Professional Growth Activity | Resources Needed | Due Date |
| --- | --- | --- |
| 1. Questioning Foundation | | |
| | | |
| | | |
| 2. Questioning Perspective | | |
| | | |
| | | |
| 3. Whole-Brain Questions | | |
| | | |
| | | |
| 4. Virtual Questions Distinctions | | |
| | | |
| | | |
| 5. Substantive In Substantive Out | | |
| | | |
| | | |

# Section II
## Planning Learning

This section is the foundation of using questions effectively. As you will repeatedly read, the largest problem with traditional questioning is that little thought is invested by the instructor prior to asking the questions. Either the questions come from the textbook or out of the instructors' own heads; they tend to be low-level questions for recalling facts. The travesty is that, often, some instructors never go beyond low-level fact-based questions.

In this section you will learn to create progressions of questions that start at low-level and then go beyond that to the high cognitive levels. If 80% of what instructors do is ask questions, then at least 80% of the planning should be about what are the best, most effective questions to ask and what is the best way to get learners to answer them.

# 6

# Wild Hog Questions

## How Do You Prepare Effective Questions Before Instruction?

### 6.1 Why Plan for Questions?

Just like the brain, the process of instruction is complicated, but if you would indulge me for a moment, I would like to set the stage for more learning in terms of syllogistic logic. If we accept that the entire purpose of "teaching" is to increase participant learning . . . and learning is categorized by how much learners remember . . . and how much learners remember is dependent on how engaged the learners are in the learning . . . then how engaged the learners are in the learning must depend on the quality of the instruction or learning delivery.[1] . . . and the quality of the learning delivery depends wholly on how well it was designed . . . then it follows that the amount of participant learning can be increased by enhancing the learning design portion of the learning cycle (see Figure 6.1). This is where WILD HOG Questions are made—while the lesson is being planned.

### 6.2 What Are WILD HOG Questions?

I will answer that question in a moment, but I will provide some background information first. Let me tell you something you may not know about Texas, one of my favorite states. It is full of wild hogs . . . millions of them! Why do you want to know this? I will get to that in a bit, but for now, I needed something that would grab your attention and imagination. Did it work?

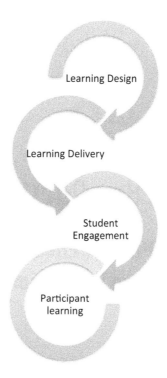

**Figure 6.1** The Process of Instruction

Anyway, to continue, these wild hogs can be quite a nuisance to farmers and ranchers, but Texans have found a way to make the best of the what could be a difficult situation. Texas landowners,[2] farmers, and ranchers have battled with these pesky hogs for many years, which has now fostered a thriving wild-hog-hunting industry.[3] Some farmers, ranchers, and other land owners, rather than simply shooting the hogs, trap them and sell them to restaurants or ship them overseas as exotic meat. Other ranchers have specialized even further by throwing up tall fences around their property and then enticing gun and bow hunters to hunt the hogs on their land for a fee.[4] More adventurous entrepreneurs take their hunter clients up in helicopters to hunt the hogs from the air.[5] Wild hog hunting in Texas is a big deal, and wild hogs are things you simply can't ignore, just like WILD HOG Questions.

Where did these hogs come from? Back when the Spaniards first came to Texas, certain numbers of domesticated hogs escaped. Later someone thought the black European wild boar would be fun to hunt and introduced those into the Texas wild. What we have today is a mix of the two. Which means, like domestic hogs, they are prolific breeders, and like the wild boar, they are tough and resilient survivors. These animals can protect themselves with their long tusks and thick hide and are extremely intelligent. Ranchers and farmers will tell you that it takes a special fence to keep wild hogs out. For regular fences, as soon as one fence gets fixed, the hogs will find a weakness someplace else. Like most hogs, they are omnivorous—i.e., they eat vegetation, insects, and meat indiscriminately, which means they are opportunistic feeders and will destroy large portions of crops and ruin harvests if left unchecked. There are estimated to be over 2.6 million wild hogs in Texas, and all the helicopter hunting, bow hunting, and live trapping has failed to diminish the population.[6] As it turns out, that could be a good thing for wild hog hunters because wild hog meat from Texas is a delicacy, much leaner and more flavorful than the pen-fed pork we buy at the supermarket.[7]

Now that you know all about wild hogs, I would like to make a comparison of the characteristics of these interesting animals to a process for developing effective questions. I will call this process WILD HOG Questioning. I need to clarify that, while WILD HOG Questions have similar properties to wild hogs, they are not known to be nuisances as are the feral pigs of Texas. Rather, they are quite beneficial for instructors and learning participants.

### Definition of WILD HOG Questions

To be specific, WILD HOG Questions are questions that, just like the feral pigs, are "in your face"; "can't be ignored"; "have to do something with them" questions. Like the wild hogs, they reproduce rapidly and multiply and create more questions. They are unpredictable, voracious, and challenging. WILD HOG Questions (not to be confused with "hog wild" questions) are also deliberate, they ignore fences, they overcome poor thinking, they are intelligent and designed to make learners think.

WILD HOG stands for *Written Intentionally for Learning Depth and Higher-Order Genius*. (OK, I know it is corny, but my family and I worked hard to come up with this acronym!) But again, the name "WILD HOG" says it all: in-your-face, challenging, unavoidable, and unpredictable (see Figure 6.2).

## 6.3  WILD HOG Questions: Written Intentionally

The *WI* in WILD stands for *Written Intentionally*. The act of writing questions must be deliberate and intentional. A question must be crafted to meet the learners' needs and the instructor's needs. Unfortunately, because in many learning

**Figure 6.2**  WILD HOG Acronym Spelled Out

situations little thought is invested in deciding beforehand what questions to ask, questioning in most situations is haphazard and, as discussed earlier, largely ineffective. Not surprisingly, these questions made "on the fly" are typically low-level questions, because that is pretty much the best you can do when you are in the middle of directing a learning activity with 30 or more learners.

Perhaps you have seen the movie *I-Robot*.[8] Will Smith, who played the character Detective Spooner, was called to an accident scene of a supposed suicide. When called to investigate Dr. Lanning's death, Detective Spooner has a conversation with a device that projects a prerecorded holograph of Dr. Alfred Lanning—the robotics genius who is recently deceased. Detective Spooner asks the holographic Dr. Lanning several low-level questions, to each of which the hologram responded, "I'm sorry. My responses are limited. You must ask the right questions." But when he asked "Why would you kill yourself?" the holograph responded, "That is the right question." Note that it is an open-ended question that gets to the heart of why Detective Spooner was there and what he really needed to investigate. In any learning situation, the "right questions" have to do the same thing: "What do I want the participants to learn?" followed closely by "How do I get them to learn it?" Low-level questions will always bring limited responses, and that is why we need to ask the right WILD HOG Questions.

While you are preparing your learning activities, it just takes a few more minutes to jot down the key Wild Hog Questions that build on each other (tiered). Crystal-clear learning objectives simplify designing and creating appropriate questions. Grant Wiggins and Jay McTighe proposed in *Understanding by Design*[9] that creating the assessment before you teach is a powerful "best practice" to increase participant learning. How are learners mainly assessed? Through questions (duh!). I propose that creating WILD HOG Questions before you ask them can also radically improve participant learning and, as a result, their performance on tests.[10] Let me explain why.

*I CANNOT EMPHASIZE THIS ENOUGH IN ORDER TO ASK GOOD, POWERFUL AND EFFECTIVE QUESTIONS, WE HAVE TO PUT SOME THOUGHT INTO THEM . . . BEFORE INSTRUCTION*

First of all, the assessment questions (we already established that tests and quizzes are made of questions) and the questions you use in class to increase learning should be the same exact questions. Why would you use one set of questions for building knowledge and then assess that knowledge with questions the participants have never heard before? Fenwick English would call that "loose alignment" of what is taught to what is tested.[11] So, if I have already created all the questions that I will use on the assessment, then the only thing I have to do is to make sure all the learners know the answers to the questions by creating learning activities that will lead them to ask and answer the questions in various situations (we'll talk more about this in Chapter 12).

Second, in group learning, I find that when I prepare the questions in advance it helps me stay focused on making sure that I have the maximum number of learners engaged, rather than trying to think up what the next question will be. To help me remember them, I write the questions I want to ask on a separate piece of paper rather than just in the lesson plan (I personally don't like carrying around my lesson plan book while I'm implementing a learning activity). 3x5 cards or a half-sheet paper work great for me. I can stick the cards in my pocket, and wherever I am in the classroom I can pull them out to refresh my memory at any time. The technologically savvy (some would say technology dependent) could jot down the WILD HOG Question on their tablet or phone and carry that around the classroom. With the questions already created, during the learning activity I can focus on the learners. Rather than frantically trying to think up the next question, I can actually listen closely as I wander about the room monitoring all the learner responses, praise or correct them accordingly, and concentrate on checking the understanding of as many learners as possible. Having the questions already decided also makes it easier when designing small-group and partner activities where the learners do the asking and answering (see Figure 6.3).

Figure 6.3 WILD HOG Questions Fundamentals

## 6.4 WILD HOG Questions: Learning Depth

LD stands for *learning depth*. You could call this rigor, but rigor is one of those "jargon" words for which the meaning is easily confused or is interpreted a multitude of ways. My interpretation of rigor is learning depth or taking basic knowledge to deeper levels through series of questions. For example, I went to the dentist, and after his initial examination the following question and answer session left me educated at deeper levels.

He said, "You have a tooth of concern."

I asked, "Why should I be concerned?"

"One tooth has a radial-luminosity at the apex of the root."

Then I asked, "What does that mean?"

He said, "The radial-luminosity at the apex of the root, or shadow at the tip of the root, could mean an infection."

"Show me," I requested

"See, here and here."

"How did that happen?"

"Your teeth are getting older and cracks open up for decay to set in."

"How can I get it fixed?"

"We'll have to put in a filling to shore up the tooth."

So, by asking questions, I helped the dentist clarify the issue and help me get at the root of the problem (sorry for the pun). Plus, I learned some terminology I didn't know before. Perhaps the most important thing about deepening learning, as illustrated in my example of the dentist and me, is to make it personal—Why do I need to know this? How can this knowledge be useful to me? This simple conversation is what I mean by rigor—or digging deeper.

Rigor is two-dimensional in that it includes difficulty and complexity. Bloom's Taxonomy (1956) and Costa's Habits of Mind (2008) relate to difficulty of thinking activities,[12] while Erickson's Concept-Based Curriculum (Erickson, Lanning, & French, 2017) relates to complexity of thinking with different types of knowledge.[13] Difficulty and complexity of thinking are different concepts. According to Bloom and Costa, difficulty in thinking refers to how much mental effort a person has to expend to think at that level. I've already explained Bloom's perspective in Section 3.2. Costa simplifies Bloom's Taxonomy into three levels, which is easier for instructors and learners to remember and use. Level one is the easiest and corresponds with Bloom's knowledge and comprehension. Level two corresponds to application and analysis, while level three includes evaluation and synthesis. Complexity of thinking regards different types of knowledge. Erickson describes a "taxonomy" of knowledge: Theory, Principle-Generalization, Concepts, Topics, and Facts. Just as with Bloom and Costa, questions must begin at the lower levels of Topics and Facts and then progress to more difficult knowledge.

Learning depth does not happen on the first question, so you have to tier (not scaffold[14]) your WILD HOG Questions from easy (level 1) to medium (level 2) and then to difficult (level 3), making sure there is a variety of questions that range also from simple (facts) to complex (theories). As an example of this, when introducing a new subject, I present vocabulary first as the basis for understanding. To help the learners identify the meaning of the words I use pictures and drawings to represent the words (see Section 8.7), and I make sure they can say the words (I found that if I can't pronounce a word, there is no way that I can remember it). Then I deepen their understanding by asking questions.

◆ I start my WILD HOG Question tier with simple recognition questions such as "touch" or "point to" the word I say.
◆ Then I ask yes or no questions. "¿Es un impermeable? (Is this a raincoat?)"
◆ Following this I move up to comparative questions. "Which is better, a raincoat or a sweater in the rain?"
◆ Then to application questions "What kind of coat do you wear when it's cold (rainy, hot, snowy)?"
◆ Finally, I asked opinion questions: "Which kind of raincoat do you prefer?" and creative or problem-solving questions: "If you have only $15, which store gives you the best value on raincoats?"

One of the things this also does is give the learner multiple opportunities (see the Rule of Three in Chapter 11) to interact with the vocabulary on several cognitive levels, enhancing their fluency and capacity to use the words and their comprehension of the terms, establishing background knowledge that serves as a staging area for new knowledge, and most importantly increasing their long-term recall (see Figure 6.4).

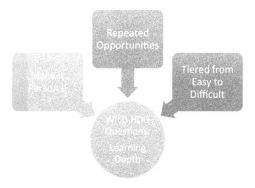

**Figure 6.4** Requirements of WILD HOG Questions: learning depth

## 6.5 WILD HOG Questions: Higher-Order Genius

HOG stands for *higher-order genius* and reminds us that including application-, analysis-, evaluation-, and synthesis-type questions will lead the learners to thinking more like the geniuses we are trying to help them become (see Section 3.2). They can't and won't ever do that with traditional questioning techniques. The success of the questioning process hinges on making sure that you have created an environment where learners feel confident that they can answer and ask questions without fear of shame or rebuke. They need to have successful learning experiences to build confidence and to think of themselves as geniuses. Answering questions in groups and partnerships lowers the affective filter (fear of embarrassment) and allows all learners to participate without having to wait for their turn. Spend time asking low-level questions and developing the knowledge, facts, and understanding, and then keep increasing the difficulty and complexity of the questions till you arrive at the highest levels Application, Analysis, Evaluation, and Creation (synthesis), Level 3, and Theories. If you look at Table 6.1, I have provided a table that correlates some question stems that illustrate a WILD HOG progression (tier) of questions using Costa's three Levels, Bloom's six levels, and Erickson's five levels.

**Table 6.1** Question Progressions Easy to Difficult

| **Rigor: Question Progression Combining Bloom, Costa, and Erickson** | |
| --- | --- |
| Costa: Level 1<br>Bloom: Knowledge and Comprehension<br>Erickson: Facts and Topics<br>(*Who, When, Where, Name, Choose, Select, Find, Restate, Define, Observe Match, Label*)<br>Convergent | Is this . . . ? What is . . . ? When did . . . ? What do . . . ? Which one . . . ? When was . . . ? How would you show . . . ? Where was . . . ? Who was . . . ? What facts . . . ? What is the definition of . . . ? How many . . . ? What is the solution for . . . ? What is the function of . . . ? What are the essential parts of . . . ? What does . . . mean? |
| Costa: Level 2<br>Bloom: Application and Analysis<br>Erickson: Concepts<br>(*How, Compare, Contrast, Inspect, Apply, Develop, Solve, Infer, Classify, Analyze, Reason, Explain, Distinguish, Examine*)<br>Convergent and Divergent | How is ___ similar to ___? How would you classify . . . ? How would you categorize . . . ? What would explain . . . ? How is ___ related to ___? How would you summarize in your own words . . . ? What steps are involved in . . . ? What characteristics do you see in . . . ? Where could you use . . . ? What is missing from . . . ? What is unique about . . . ? To which group does . . . belong? |

## Rigor: Question Progression Combining Bloom, Costa, and Erickson

| | |
|---|---|
| Costa: Level 3<br>Bloom: Evaluation and Synthesis<br>Erickson: Generalizations, Principles, Theories<br>(*Why, Evaluate, Judge, Criticize, Assess, Predict, Forecast, Create, Infer, Imagine, Prove, Reflect, Resolve*)<br>Divergent | Why do you think . . . ? What would you infer from . . . ? What conclusions have you made? What judgment could be made about . . . ? Which is the best answer? What would you predict if . . . ? How would you prioritize . . . ? What would you do if you could . . . ? Why was . . . better than . . . ? How could you prove or disprove . . . ? What evidence supports . . . ? What are some alternatives? What comes to mind when you reflect . . . ? What intrigued you so much that . . . ? How could you improve . . . ? What would you to do fix . . . ? How could you design a better . . . ? |

Since you will create your own higher-order genius question progression (tier), you also need to address the other half of the equation: the genius answers. Half of creating wonderful questions is training the learner to answer them (see Chapter 14). You should not leave this up to chance. Let them know, and "train" them on how to respond appropriately before asking the questions. For example, they need to know that answering questions in complete sentences, orally and in writing, is an effective communication tool, and it forces clarity of thinking. As discussed in Chapter 5, they need to know your standards of substantiveness: how long the response is, what kind of evidence they need to provide, etc. One of the things that I had to "train" my learners to do is work in partners, trios, and groups. Without this training, group work was chaos to be avoided. Within the instructions, I provided exactly what each person was supposed to do and what each person was responsible for accomplishing in the group. The first times you do this, it will take a few more minutes, but as you continue group work, it will become more routine, and participants will know what to do.

### Creating Classroom Climate

First of all, the classroom climate has to be one in which learners are willing to take risks. Some learners may feel comfortable asking questions no matter where they are, but most are hesitant to put themselves out there unless they feel secure: security from the instructor they respect and fear but most importantly security from their fellow classmates. They have to know each other well enough to know how they will respond—you see it is not just what happens in the classroom but interactions outside of the classroom and in other classes that matter. At this point, I must be a realist. Because of these factors, it is impossible to engage every learner the same way. For some learners the only engagement you will get is minimal. At least it is engagement.

There are some things the instructor can control. It's easy enough to establish classroom rule:; no teasing or laughing at other learner's questions, placing placards on the wall: "There is no such thing as a dumb question," but forcing engagement will only bring passive compliance at best and active resistance at worst. In normal situations, the instructor cannot just hand things over to a bunch of brilliant learners and say "Figure it out" (Montessori method: unadulterated and pure learner-centered learning). Allowing learners to take complete control of the Socratic Seminar or debate will lead to those learners who demand attention, those that are the loudest, etc. co-opting the learning experience of most of the other learners. So, we turn to cooperative groups and project-based learning to divide and conquer.

## Establishing Genius-Level Climate Through Group Work.

We call it "group work" when instructors divide the class into small groups and give the learners tasks to perform. Let's be honest here. Some learners hate group work with a passion, while others love it. It is interesting to note which learners love which and why. The scholarly learners detest "working in groups" because they see right through it as augmented busywork. They get little from it and, more often than not, they end up doing the lion's share of the work if they are placed in "heterogenous" groups as instructors are so fond of doing. The less-dedicated learners love group work because it gives them time to be more social and get easy sympathy grades for almost no work. Instructors love group work too because it keeps the learners "engaged" (busy), and instead of having to grade 30 projects per class, they only have to six or seven.

Group work that creates a learning environment where learners feel comfortable asking questions requires three things:

1  A viable, challenging, open-ended question (or questions) to answer
2  Specific and clearly communicated standards of performance
3  Specific and clearly communicated roles with associated individual responsibility.

The best way to get the learners to learn to overcome years of "wait till I tell you what to do" training is to not tell them exactly "what" to do, but give them a direction and parameters on "how" to achieve success.[15] This won't be easy at first because learners aren't used to it and have been trained to do the exact opposite for years. Trust me. They will catch on after several tries. Table 6.2 is a sample WILD HOG Question Rubric template that you

**Table 6.2** WILD HOG Question Sample Rubric

| | | WILD HOG Rubric | |
|---|---|---|---|
| **Topic: Sovereignty and Suzerainty** | | | |
| **The students will effectively answer the following questions:** | | **Possible Grade** | |
| | **A level** | **B Level** | **C Level** |
| Content Knowledge | How can you show what sovereignty is and what suzerainty is? | How can you explain sovereignty and suzerainty? | What does sovereignty mean? What does suzerainty mean? |
| Concept Understanding | What are the characteristics and actual effects of sovereignty and suzerainty? | What are the characteristics and intended effects of sovereignty and suzerainty? | What are the characteristics of sovereignty and suzerainty? |
| Application of Concepts | What are some examples and non- examples of sovereignty and suzerainty, and how do they compare with the historical examples found in the world? | What are some examples and non- examples of sovereignty and suzerainty? | What examples of sovereignty and suzerainty exist today? |
| Analysis of Concepts | What are the pro's and cons of sovereignty and suzerainty? | What are the similarities and differences of sovereignty and suzerainty? | What is the difference between sovereignty and suzerainty? |
| Evaluation of Concepts | What is the balance between the US and the 50 states in maintaining individual sovereignty and limiting suzerainty. | Which is more effective, Sovereignty or Suzerainty for individual well being? …for the government? | Why do some prefer, Sovereignty over Suzerainty? |
| Synthesis of Concepts | What international groups threaten the US sovereignty today and what should we do about it? | Is Puerto Rico sovereign, suzerain, or both. What would you suggest to them as a course of action in the future? | What did the founders of the Constitution have to say about sovereignty and suzerainty? |

can easily transform into a rubric to provide for the participants so they can gauge their own progress toward success.

## 6.6 The WILD HOG Question Process of Creation

Let me show you how I would create WILD HOG Questions in preparation for a math lesson for sixth grade: multiplying fractions. Before I start preparing for this lesson, I have three concerns: 1) My first concern is that I have to realize that there needs to be an application or purpose for why we would ever want to multiply fractions,[16] 2) not all of the learners will remember what fractions and ratios are, so I may have to review the concepts, and 3) not all the learners will remember the mechanics of dealing with fractions, so we might have to review the process steps. I need to check for understanding to find out how much the learners know so that I can address these concerns.

To solve the first concern, since learners need and deserve to know how useful this skill is, we can turn to science and medicine to provide several possibilities. One example comes to mind. One of the problems that hospital nurses have to do frequently is convert a prescription into a dosage. The nurse is the one responsible for figuring out how to get the right dosage for the patient and may have to compute different proportions, units, ratios of mixtures, or even different prescriptions that need to be calculated. For example, the bottle in the medicine cabinet might say 500 grams per milliliter of the drug, but the doctor writes a prescription for the patient for 750 milligrams per pound (weight of the patient) per every six hours. The nurse would have to convert the grams to milligrams and milliliters and then figure out how many milliliters of solution per pound the patient needs every six hours. This is all done through multiplying fractions and ratios.[17] Another example is the idea of baking and cooking. Each recipe has different fractions that need to adjusted to the number of people, enlarging the recipe or cutting the recipe to fit the group. The more relevant the example application of the concept, the better. I think I will use the second example because it matches the level of sixth grader skills and interests more closely.

For the second concern, before I can have learners multiplying fractions, they need to understand that this is different from adding and subtracting fractions. I also need learners to comprehend that percents and ratios are also fractions. Just reteaching it as if they had never heard of fractions before will waste your time and theirs. A simple review found on the internet could refresh the learners' memories.[18] After that, a series of review questions would be in order. The following are some knowledge and fact-based questions I could use to find out what they remember:

> "Raise your hand if you remember how to add and subtract fractions."
>> "Stand up if you know how to multiply fractions."
>> "Thumbs up if you think a ratio is a fraction, thumbs down if you don't. Ask your elbow partner, 'Why do you think that way?'"
>> "Thumbs up if a percent is a fraction, thumbs down if not. Ask your elbow partner, 'Why do you think that way?'"
>> "Stand up if you feel that both ratios and percents are fractions."

The final concern is that learners will need to understand the mechanics of multiplication of fractions and make sure they remember the details of fractions . . . i.e. a review of the vocabulary (denominator, numerator, dividend, quotient, ratio, etc.). The best way to do this is to make a competition or game out of it. The old standbys such as the Jeopardy reverse questions; they give you the "answer" and you come up with the question, usually, "What is . . . (the definition of the answer)?" or other game-show set of questions may be good for older learners. Younger ones are going to need something more interactive like a relay race where they are given a question and need to run to find the matching card and bring it back before the other team does (older learners like this too). These are good for low-level learning, but asking a question, "How could you explain the rules of multiplying fractions in a rap dance?" takes it to a higher level of learning. You might get something like this: *numerator to numerator, boom boom, denominator to denominator, boom boom, right across the top and right across the bottom, yeah . . .* (see Section 13.5). Learners can come up with some cool (cooler than mine) songs if you let them. The learners can choreograph it with actions to the words that make sense as to what they are doing, but the most important thing is that they are doing it, and for that reason they will remember it.[19] Below are some questions I might ask to check for understanding and see if they understand the mechanics:

> "What is one-half plus one-half? If you know the answer raise your left elbow in the air. Now tell your neighbor the answer. Everyone who got 'one' as the answer stand up."
>> "What is one-half times one-half? If you know the answer raise your right elbow. Now tell your other neighbor. Everyone who got 'one-fourth' as the answer stand up."
>> "With your partner, describe what the difference is between adding fractions and multiplying fractions."

"What would be a rule you could create about adding fractions? What is a rule about multiplying fractions?"

"Ask your elbow partner, "How would I write four parts water and six parts flour as a ratio? Everyone, point to the answer on the whiteboard."

"Ask your elbow partner, "How would I write 75% as a fraction? Now thumbs up if the answer is correct on the whiteboard, or thumbs down if it is upside down."

## Moving From Convergent to Divergent

Now that I have thought and prepared questions for resolving these initial concerns, I am ready to start creating more advanced questions. As you noticed earlier, most knowledge, comprehension questions are convergent, meaning that there is only one correct answer. If I ask, "Is this an MPU?" or "What is an endoplasmic reticulum?"[20] I'm expecting a particular answer. These questions are also known as "closed" questions and can usually be answered in a word, short phrase, or sentence. divergent—or "open-ended"—questions cannot be answered in one word, and they have many possible answers. Divergent questions require more thought and more planning. For this reason, I created a simple spreadsheet table (see Table 6.3) to help me record my questions and to keep track of the question tiers from easy to difficult, simple to complex. The table also tracks the types of questions I am looking for, if there is only one answer (convergent), or if there are multiple answers and any of them would be acceptable (divergent) (see Figure 6.5).[21] I know, it seems like a lot of work in addition to the planning and preparation required for teaching. Believe me, the effort is worth it in time saved from having to reteach and retrench. Over time, it gets easier, and you will start to create muscle memory

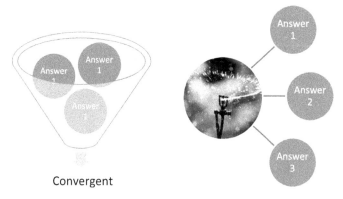

Convergent

**Figure 6.5** Convergent vs Divergent

**Table 6.3** WILD HOG Questions Worksheet

| Costa Level | Erikson Level | Convergent (Only one correct answer) | Divergent (Many plausible answers) | Audience |
|---|---|---|---|---|
| 1 Gathering info | Facts | What is… | How do… | Individual |
| 2 Analyzing info | Topics | Where is… | Why does… | One on One |
| 3 Judging/Applying info | Concepts | When is… | What if… | Elbow partners |
| | Generalizations | How is… | | Threesome |
| | Principles | | | Small group |
| | | | | Four Corner groups |
| | | | | Divided class |
| | | | | All at once |

Lesson Topic: _Multiplying Fractions_          Date _____

| Questions | Bloom's Objective | Costa Level | Erikson Level | Convergent | Divergent | For Which Students? |
|---|---|---|---|---|---|---|
| Raise your hand if you know what is a fraction.- Ok, now tell your neighbor. | Define Fraction | 1 | Facts | What is a fraction? | | Elbow partner |
| Ask your elbow partner, "How is that different from a ratio?" | Analysis | 2 | Concepts | How are fractions and ratios different? | | Elbow partner |
| Stand up If you can name the parts of a fraction. Ask your other elbow partner to name them. | Define Fraction | 1 | Facts | What are the parts of a fraction? | | Elbow partner |

Continued

Table 6.3 WILD HOG Questions Worksheet (cont.)

| Questions | Bloom's Objective | Costa Level | Erikson Level | Convergent | Divergent | For Which Students? |
|---|---|---|---|---|---|---|
| On your table, Can you discover an easy way to remember which is which? | Compare and contrast | 2 | Generalizations | | How do tell them apart? | Small group |
| When you add fractions you have to find the lowest common denominator, what about when you multiply fractions? On your personal white boards write the steps you take to multipy fractions. | Compare and Constrast | 2 | Generalizations | What is different? | | Individual |
| Ask your elbow partner what happens when I multiply one half times one half? | Application, Analysis | 3 | Generalizations | | What if | Elbow partner |
| So one half of one half is one quarter. What happens when I multiply 2/3 by ½? How did you get that? Raise your personal white boards to show your work. Teach your elbow partner what you learned. | Application | 3 | Generalizations Principals | | What does, How do | All at once Elbow partner |
| Is 2/6 half of 2/3? Let's check. On your personal white boards… Convert 2/3 to sixths. Discuss with your partner how to do that. What is the answer? What is half of that? Does it match? | Application Evaluation | 3 | Generalizations Principals | | What does, How do | All at once Elbow partner |

on creating effective questions for each scenario, content, and learner. Here are my more advanced questions examples:

> "Let's say that I am inviting friends over for a pizza party and the rec- ipe for one pizza requires three-quarters cups of flour, but I will need three pizzas. How much flour should I make sure I have? In your trio, use what you know about fractions and find a solution."
>
> "If I make rice with a ratio of three to one, how much water do I add if I have one-half cup rice? In your trio think of two ways to solve the problem."
>
> "You find the socks of your dreams, and they are on sale. The tag says to take off 10% of the original price, but there is a sign that says take off an additional 5%. If the socks cost $10 originally, what is the total discounted price? In your trio, write a procedure that tells how you solve this problem."
>
> "In your trio, think of a business that uses fractions, ratios, and percents, and identify in what situations these would be used."
>
> The following figures represents convergent vs divergent—funnel vs sprinkler.

## Consider the Learner

Along with types of questions, we also need to consider the learner. As much as I think I am egalitarian in my questioning, if I don't decide to whom I will ask the question beforehand, I tend to throw the questions out to the whole class and you know the rest of the story (only the learners who know or think they know the answer will listen or participate in any way). Additionally, thinking "who is going to answer the question?" can also help customize the question to the needs and interests of particular learners (see Chapter 7, Sections 8.6 and 8.7). It is paramount that, in whatever questioning process I use, I somehow bring it back to engaging every learner. While I do not believe that whole-group questions are effective, if, by chance, I begin with a single selected learner to answer a question, then, before I am done, I need to get every learner to answer that same question. This could be as simple as, "Now turn to your elbow partner and ask the same question" or as complex as a jigsaw trainer of trainers exercise. There is no reason you can't start with part- ners and small groups . . . but I know, old habits.

## Writing the Questions

The first thing is to get the questions down on paper (or a spreadsheet), so you can look at them. Once I have brainstormed a list of questions, if I keep the objective of the learning events clearly set in my mind, I can refine and eliminate any questions that don't contribute or that might lead the learners down the wrong thought pathways. I provided an example of a history lesson on sovereignty and suzerainty[22] and a blank table at the end of this chapter to help you make sure that you have questions in each of Bloom's categories and in each of Costa's difficulty Levels (see Table 6.2 WILD HOG Question Developer). Then put I must put myself in the shoes of the learner and try to determine how they will respond to the questions. To do so, I need to answer the following questions:

◆ Do the learners know the answers—or at least how to get the answer?
◆ Are the questions Zombie Questions (too easy, or begging the question [i.e. "What color is George Washington's white horse?"] see Chapter 12)?
◆ Are the questions convergent (i.e. there is only one right answer)?
◆ Which questions lead the learners to divergent thinking (i.e. there are multiple correct answers, but perhaps some answers are better than others)?[23]
◆ How do I make sure that the maximum number of learners is engaged with these questions?

To show you how writing WILD HOG Questions works, I have an example of a question progression sheet for creating and keeping track of your WILD HOG Questions (see Table 6.3), and you can find a blank spreadsheet after Table 6.3. We are going to be revisiting the WILD HOG Question creation process throughout this book and looking in more detail about using WILD HOG Questions, but you now have the gist. The best thing about creating WILD HOG Questions as you plan your lessons is that the process makes the lesson flow and in essence is your lesson. There is one more caveat. With the WILD HOG Questions already written, you have all you need for your examinations, quizzes, or tests. The following is a summary of what we learned about WILD HOG Questions in this chapter.

## Summary
1  WILD HOG Questions stands for _written intentionally for learning depth and higher-order genius._
2  WILD HOG Questions are written intentionally:
   a  Written before instruction
   b  Perfect alignment to learning objectives
   c  Easy to hard/simple to complex
   d  Balanced convergent vs divergent
   e  Engage the maximum number of learners.

3   WILD HOG Questions are designed for learning depth, and learning depth requires rigor composed of difficulty and complexity. Bloom and Costa define difficulty, while Erickson identifies complexity.
    a   Make it personal
    b   Repeated opportunities
    c   Tiered from easy to difficult.
4   WILD HOG Questions promote higher-order genius:
    a   Creating genius-friendly questions that create a learning environment where learners feel comfortable asking questions requires three things:
        i    A viable, challenging, open-ended question (divergent) to answer
        ii   Specific and clearly communicated standards of performance
        iii  Specific and clearly communicated roles with associated individual responsibility.
5   Writing WILD HOG Questions requires thought about where the participants are and the creation of questions to check for understanding, anticipating that some might need more than the rest of the class.
6   WILD HOG Questions begin with low-level, convergent questions, then progress to higher-level, divergent questions.
7   In preparation for the lesson, also think about who do you want to be answering these questions. Particularly designing questions to match interests and needs of individual learners is a powerful learning tool.
8   Because there are so many questions to keep track of, it helps to use a form that makes sure that you tier the questions from easy to difficult and from simple to complex. Done correctly, you have created not only the entire lesson but also the evaluation.

## Questions to Consider

1   What effect will writing the questions as you plan your lesson have on your instruction?

_____

_____

_____

2   How will I push my learners to deeper thinking in order to increase learning?

_____

_____

_____

3   What do I think the largest obstacle for achieving learning depth in my instruction would be?

_____

_____

_____

In the content area that we are studying write questions for:
   a   Costa's Level 1

_____

_____

_____

   b   Costa's Level 2

_____

_____

_____

   c   Costa's Level 3

_____

_____

_____

5   What changes will I have to make in my instruction in order to develop higher-order genius?

_____

_____

_____

6   In the content area we are studying, what kind of questions can I write?
   a   Convergent

_____

_____

_____

   b   Divergent

_____

_____

_____

7 Take some time and write your own WILD HOG Question Progression in a topic you are studying now.

_____

_____

_____

_____

_____

_____

_____

_____

_____

_____

_____

_____

## Notes

1  I want to be completely clear about my intent by avoiding the use of the word "teach." If we want schools to dramatically improve student academic performance, we have to change the way we look at education. The word "teach" has too many cultural memories that involve traditional teacher-directed learning. So, in this book, I will be using "learn" as the main focus of our attention, hence "learning delivery" instead of teaching. If I could arrange it, I would eliminate entirely the word "teacher" in favor of "learning engineer" (see my blog post of June 28th of 2013 at www.edutopia.org, entitled, "Great Teachers Don't Teach").

2  97% of the land in Texas is private. You would think that, in a state as large as Texas, there would be a great deal of "public" land, but there is an interesting reason there is not. The history of Texas land extends back to the Spanish colonies when Moses F. Austin was granted permission to settle 300 American families in the 1820s. His son Stephen F. Austin developed the land from modern Austin to Houston. The Spanish and later Mexican land system granted plots of land to private citizens, and basically all the land in Texas was thus divided and privatized. Texas landowners vehemently protected and expanded their holding—King Ranch, for example, was developed that way. It is the largest ranch in the United states (825,000 acres in 6 different properties).

3 Hunting on private property requires no hunting license. Also, because hogs are classified as a nuisance, anyone can hunt them without a license on public land and private land.

4 *American Hoggers 2011*: www.imdb.com/title/tt1988897/

5 "Helicopter Hog Hunting": www.youtube.com/watch?v=-7piaK4F4N4

6 For an interesting investigation about feral hogs in Texas, Texas Parks and Wildlife has an informative article under the heading of Nuisance Wildlife in Texas. https://tpwd.texas.gov/huntwild/wild/nuisance/feral_hogs/; here are some other sites so that you can find out everything you want to know about wild hogs in Texas: https://agrilifeextension.tamu.edu/solutions/feral-hogs/, https://countryrebel.com/texas-over-run-with-feral-hogs-hunt-365-days-a-year/

7 Where to get wild hog meat: www.texasspecialtymeats.com/

8 *I, Robot* is a 2004 science fiction/action film directed by Alex Proyas and produced by 20th Century Fox. *I, Robot* is a movie based on the ground-breaking book by Isaac Azimov by the same name. Azimov set up three hierarchical mandates that maintain human superiority over robots. The movie takes this idea and shows how humans and robots are being harmed. For the clip mentioned, see: www.youtube.com/watch?v=Nx8LAFSY3Ws; for the transcript see: www.imdb.com/title/tt0343818/quotes?item=qt0474820

9 Aside from their landmark book *Understanding by Design* written in 2005, Vanderbilt University's Center for Teachers has an excellent module on UBD: https://cft.vanderbilt.edu/guides-sub-pages/understanding-by-design/ (but, interestingly enough, no modules on asking questions).

10 In an interview with Dr. Grant Wiggins, I had the chance to ask him how well the concept of "backwards design" (i.e. creating the evaluation before the instruction) has caught on. He was reserved in his comment, but his disappointment was obvious: "not as well as we might hope" was his answer. You can read the interview on Edutopia.org under my blog for November of 2013. Dr. Wiggins passed away in 2015.

11 Fenwick English is a professor at University of North Carolina at Chapel Hill, UNC Educational Leadership and is the alignment king. He draws on the shape of the triangle formed by what is to be taught, what is actually taught, and what is tested. He proposes that it should be exactly the same. See https://unc.academia.edu/FenwickEnglish

12 Arthur Costa simplified Blooms in a way that students can understand and remember, a hierarchy of difficulty in asking questions. For more information see: www.habitsofmindinstitute.org/ and www.lansing-schools.org/tfiles/folder1342/Costa%20%26%20Kallick,%202015%20Five%20

Strategies%20for%20Questioning%20with%20Intention.pdf Costa, A (2008), "Learning and Leading with Habits of Mind," ASCD: Alexandria, VA.

13  H. Lyn Erickson is the "godmother" of concept-based curriculum. The idea that concept knowledge transfers but not factual knowledge is foundational to her theories. If learners understand one concept, they can transfer that knowledge or generalize it to other situations. Erickson, H. L., Lanning, L. A., & French, R. (2017). *Concept-based curriculum and instruction for the thinking classroom* (2nd ed.). Corwin a SAGE Publishing Company. ISBN 9781506355399.

14  Scaffolding is a term commonly used in construction. When building a wall or renovating a building, temporary structures are placed on the outside of the building so that the workers can easily access the walls as they are repaired or built. Scaffolding questions could be used in similar fashion. Scaffolding questions allow the student to build knowledge. They are probing questions, clarification questions, and questions that lead students to new understanding.

15  I had the privilege of working for the Ford partnership for academic success (PAS) program. During the course of a summer, I witnessed the transformation of 30 incoming ninth graders from passive learners to active learners. At the end of the six-week summer program, their attitudes and behaviors had changed from "I'll wait for you to tell me what should do and what I should learn" to "I have an idea, let me get with my group and see if we can make it work." The Ford PAS program curriculum is inquiry-based and cross-disciplinary and built on project-based learning principles. Now you can find it under the umbrella of Ford Next Generation Learning, and it is even better. Check it out at http://fordngl.com/

16  In 2011, Howard Crumpton and Anne Gregory did some research about relevancy and at-risk students (what student is not at risk for something?). Their determination from their longitudinal study of 44 students over 2 years (2006–2008) was that the more a student felt that what they were learning was useful, the more engaged they were in learning it. They also found that neither extrinsic nor intrinsic motivation was enough to raise grades significantly: http://eric.ed.gov/?id=EJ906535.

17  I learned how to do this first from my wife who is studying nursing. I then watched a Khan Academy video on how to do the calculations (see www.khanacademy.org/math/cc-sixth-grade-math/cc-6th-ratios-prop-topic/cc-6th-unit-conversion/v/unit-conversion-example—drug-dosage). Finally, I found a great resource that I could point students to: Medical Dosage Calculations for Dummies (see www.dummies.com/how-to/content/medical-dosage-calculations-for-dummies-cheat-shee.html)

18  www.coolmath.com/prealgebra/01-fractions/fractions-01-what-are-they-01.htm

19  I saw a fourth-grade science class do this with pretty complex subjects such as solvents, machines, and the geology of the earth. The teacher exposed the students to professionally made songs about science, and the participants learned the words and put their own actions to the words. Later, the students made their own chants/songs/raps about new scientific concepts. What was cool was that every student was able to sing the songs. I watched them take a test and, sure enough, they began dancing in their seats. Their arms, legs, and hands began retracing the mental pathways to well-learned knowledge as they answered the questions.

20  An MPU could be a microprocessor unit or a multiprocessor unit or several other things I wasn't thinking about. The endoplasmic reticulum is an organelle in eukaryotic cells (cells with a defined nucleus) that creates and transports protein.

21  I read a design proposal for a convergent and divergent software program that seeks to increase creativity by helping users tap into databases that promote both divergent and convergent thinking. Their research indicates also that convergent thinking has a tendency to interfere with divergent thinking if that is the only stimulus: *Leaving the Beaten Tracks in Creative Work—A Design Theory for Systems that Support Convergent and Divergent Thinking* (Müller-Wienbergen, Müller, Seidel, & Becker, 2011). I don't think anyone has created it yet; it seems like it would be a valuable tool.

22  For an interesting perspective of American sovereignty, please read *Why Does Sovereignty Matter to America?* by Steven Groves: www.heritage.org/research/reports/2010/12/why-does-sovereignty-matter-to-america?mb=true#form_anchor

23  I had an interesting conversation with my 16-year-old daughter about her public school experience with Convergence and Divergence. She felt that, often, the use of cooperative learning, group work, and project-based learning was like putting a square peg into a round hole—it just doesn't fit, and she hates it. She hated having to work in groups, do Socratic Seminars, and other often-utilized "student-centered" techniques. Having espoused that these techniques were the saviors of public education, this revelation caused me great concern until she explained further. Some classes like math, science, English, and social studies all expected a correct answer (Convergent), whereas her art, acting, voice and dance classes did not expect one correct answer (Divergent). She had no problems working in groups doing Divergent thinking in classes where one correct answer was not required.

# References

Bloom, B. S. (1956). *Taxonomy of educational objectives, handbook I: The cognitive domain*. New York: David McKay Co Inc.

Costa, A (2008). *Learning and leading with habits of mind*. Alexandria, VA: Association for Supervision and Curriculum Development.

Erickson, H. L., Lanning, L. A., & French, R. (2017). *Concept-based curriculum and instruction for the thinking classroom* (2nd ed.). Corwin a SAGE Publishing Company. ISBN 9781506355399.

Müller-Wienbergen, F., Müller, O., Seidel, S., & Becker, J. (2011). Leaving the beaten tracks in creative work—A design theory for systems that support convergent and divergent thinking. *Journal of the Association for Information Systems*, 12(11), 714–740. doi:10.17705/1jais.00280

# 7

# A Question for Every Brain

## How Do You Differentiate Questions According to Needs?

When I was a new teacher, I remember looking at my roll sheet and seeing multiple letters after several students' names. I asked colleagues what the abbreviations stood for and soon learned that the common perspective was that they stood for more work and more trouble. These letters represented students with exceptional learning needs, learning difficulties, behavior difficulties, or language difficulties. Whatever age you are called to inspire to learn, you have a range of capacities and needs in your participant group, and you must try to fulfil their needs.

These acronyms were supposed to help me differentiate instruction—or vary a lesson—to meet the needs of these learners. I remember struggling to grasp how I was supposed to accommodate for all participant learning without sacrificing high academic standards. I questioned how I could give the advanced learner what she needed while at the same time fulfilling the needs of the struggling learner. I also remember thinking to myself how much easier it would be to just have the "good learners." It wasn't until later that I fully realized that the reason I wanted to be an educator was not to have an easy ride but to make a difference in learners' lives. And the greatest difference I could make was in the life of one of those acronym kids. That's when "teaching" became fun.

## 7.1 Know Your Learners

In this transformation, I learned that getting to know the participants in my class was essential. Observing their behaviors comes naturally, and I quickly discover who are the eager beaver learners, who are the recalcitrant learners, and who are the quiet, observant ones. Obtaining information about their interests and skills in order to create valuable learning connections requires asking questions. I'm not saying we need to pry into their lives, but noticing things and asking them about them is perfectly alright. If a learner has a tennis racket sticking out of her backpack, you can ask, "How is tennis going?" and start learning about this. Later in your planning, you can include tennis examples, which will make a connection with that—particular learner.

You will be interested in reading more about differentiation from the queen of creating multiple learning paths, Carol Ann Tomlinson. In the book she wrote with Jay McTighe, *Integrating Differentiated Instruction and Understanding by Design*,[1] she makes clear the point that simply having activities that differentiate learning is not enough: "Differentiated instruction focuses on whom we teach, where we teach, and how we teach. Its primary goal is ensuring that teachers focus on processes and procedures that ensure effective learning for varied individuals." Deliberately designing WILD HOG Questions is the real key to increasing the understanding of all learners.

## 7.2   Group Learning Is the Key to Differentiated Instruction

Differentiation for each participant is nearly impossible to do in a "whole-class" situation. The key is to break up the class into small groups of two, three, or four. In regard to group work, I was lucky because I had been trained as a Spanish instructor, and working with partners and small groups was natural. I was well practiced in thematic instruction, and teaching a language lends itself to project-based learning and performance-based instruction; both are active-learning strategies that naturally differentiate and require groups. I learned that one of the best ways to differentiate is to simply allow it to happen in small groups. Asking differentiated questions to a whole classroom doesn't make sense, because there is no way to do it without wasting time and effort, but targeting learner needs through small groups is not only manageable, but it is the best way to differentiate.

### Composing the Groups
Small-group questioning is ideal for differentiated instruction because the group has to work out what is the best answer for each member through discussion among the members of the group, which really would not happen in a whole-class "discussion" (see Chapter 6, Creating Classroom Climate). In choosing participants in the groups, at first, my training led me to match the advanced learners with struggling learners so that they could help each other

(heterogeneous groups). I noticed after a while that if I split up the learners that way, group mentalities would emerge, and the struggling learners soon ceased struggling. They became content to let the more advanced kids do the work. So, I mixed it up—randomly, homogenously, and heterogeneously. I mixed groups by height, by alphabet, by what they liked on their pizza, their favorite ice cream, and even their answers on a four-choice question. I also, for targeted instruction, purposefully grouped learners with similar skill sets, needs, interests, or character traits. Part of my decision to do this came from having a long conversation with my youngest daughter about group work. She hated it because her instructors would always put her with the low-achieving students and she would end up doing all the work.

I discovered some very positive side effects from mixing groups randomly or homogenously. I noticed that learners who would normally not say anything or rarely participate in a heterogeneous group all of the sudden developed leadership skills and took on responsibility in a way I had never seen them demonstrate before. When I placed learners with their peers of similar skills and attitudes, I assigned questions that they would take turns asking and answering. These were the WILD HOG Questions that I had created during lesson preparation. The group that was struggling with English received questions that were less complex (see Section 8.7) but the same content, while the group full of high-achieving learners had the opposite. Because of the lower affective filter,[2] increased learner inquiry in those groups promoted differentiation of learning. When a learner is asking questions, those questions are automatically going to be at his or her cognitive level. The best part about small group questioning activities is that the learners help each other find the answers at their own level according to their own needs.

## 7.3 Options for Differentiation

Effective instructors throughout time have always found ways to reach individual learners through questions. The following are some question design options that we have in order to differentiate for our learners' needs.

- ◆ You can vary the length or quantity of the questions.
- ◆ You can extend or curtail the duration of the questions.
- ◆ You can change the language of the questions.
- ◆ You can adjust the complexity of the questions.
- ◆ You can tier the questions from hard to medium to easy.
- ◆ You can ask questions about things they know.

As you prepare your WILD HOG Questions, it takes just a moment to identify which questions would be best for which kind of learners. Identify which participants should answer these questions in the audience column of the WILD HOG Question Progression form in Chapter 6.

## Summary

1   Differentiation is attempting to meet the varied needs of all learners by adjusting the instructional strategies.
2   In order to do this, the instructor must get to know the learners' behavior characteristics as well as their skills and interests.
3   Group work facilitates differentiation automatically because the learners interact with members of the group on their own levels.
4   Groups do not always have to be heterogeneous with advanced learners and struggling learners together. Benefits arise from mixing the groups randomly and homogenously.
5   In creating WILD HOG Questions, instructors have a limited number of things that can be adjusted for individualized learning, which can be targeted to particular participants.

## Questions to Consider

1   What differentiated learning needs exist among my learners?

_____

_____

_____

_____

_____

_____

_____

_____

2   As I list them, in my current instruction, what questions will I pose for them?

_____

_____

_____

_____

_____

_____

_____

_____

_____

_____

## Notes

1   Tomlinson, C. A., & McTighe, J. (2006). *Integrating differentiated instruction and understanding by design*. Alexandria, VA: Association for Supervision and Curriculum Development.
2   Affective filters are emotions that stop certain behaviors that cause emotional responses like embarrassment, fear of ridicule, fear of failure etc. When people are placed in situations that cause these kinds of emotions, most refuse to participate. If they have to, they will be incapable of performing at their level because of the cortisol flowing through their brains, effectively shutting them down. Such a traumatic experience will only make things worse for the learner. Partner or group work is a way to reduce the affective filter and make it easier for full participation.

## Reference

Tomlinson, C. A., & McTighe, J. (2006). *Integrating differentiated instruction and understanding by design*. Alexandria, VA: Association for Supervision and Curriculum Development.

# 8

# Questions 101

## What Are Effective Ways to Write Questions?

## 8.1 Creating Authentic Questions

### Know Something About Your Participants

Authentic questions begin with being authentic. Your learners can tell if you pulled the question right out of the book or if the question is one of those "standardized" questions they will be seeing on the state exam. An authentic question is one that tells the learners that you know something about them. The first type of authentic question is personalized for particular learners. This doesn't mean simply say their name or use them in an example, though that is a good start; it means that either the question is something they know about, have personal interest in, or have experience with. In order to do this, you need to get to know who is in your group. A simple three-question survey will be enough: What is your hobby? What do you read? What music do you like? A survey like this will give you enough information to customize questions for any age. For younger learners you can do it verbally or ask the parents about their child. Let's say you are learning about Socrates, and, according to your survey, one of your learners has an interest in skateboarding. Here is an example of what you could say to make the question relevant to that learner and the other learners.

"When someone does not want to answer a question, you could say they 'skate' around the answer. Why was Socrates the first skater? Discuss this question with your partners and see if you both can come up with an answer."

If they know something about Socrates, then they may come up with, "Socrates was the first skater because when poor Plato asked a question, Socrates would never answer it, but would ask another question!"

Yes, I know. I'm stretching it thin, but that is the type of question that at least those skaters will particularly remember. It is also corny enough to be a memorable question for all of the learners because it is unique and also because it shows that you took some time to relate the information to them. If you know that you have a bunch of engineering majors in your classroom, you will gain their attention if you put your questions in terms that they are studying.

## Know What Is Relevant to Them

Current events are perfect ways get your questions to relate directly to your learners. Whether it be what is happening in the news or what is happening after school, you can weave this information into questions that will make them think. For example, in a writing lesson on cause and effect, in areas where there is a large skiing population, like Utah, you could bring up the snow report and create questions regarding the relationship between the current snowfall and the effect on the opening dates of the ski resorts, tourism, local economies, water supply, or travel. Weaving those things into your questioning and connecting them with the content you are studying will bring relevance to the learning.

## The Question Makes the Connection to Other Learning

I'm not talking about teaching your learners how to solve the Pythagorean Theorem so you can then ask questions about the Egyptian pyramids.[1] One of the best ways to make connections to other learning, without having to teach them, is to make references to the other learning and knowledge through allusions, metaphors, and similes. I am an action movie fan, and in the first *Avengers* movie (2012), Captain America (Chris Evans) cannot keep up with the references and allusion because he was asleep for 70 years. They have gathered the team and are having a discussion on what to do. Nick Fury (Samuel L. Jackson) makes an allusion to the Wizard of Oz by referencing "flying monkeys" and Thor (Chris Hemsworth) says, "Monkeys, I do not understand," and Captain America pipes up and says, "I do! I understood that reference!"[2] Lesson learned: use allusions that everyone will understand. Let's say you are doing a seminar on financial resiliency. You don't have to explain the entire message of the song, "Feed the Birds"[3] from the movie *Mary Poppins* (1964), all you have to do is reference it by mentioning "Tuppence a bag," unless you are questioning the younger generation, and then you might have to show them the clip before you use the reference.

## Learners Need to Do Something

In making authentic questions, the final point I want to make is that simply asking a question may be enough to inspire your learners to think, but the most powerful way to get them thinking is to ask the question in a way that requires them to do something useful. For example, you can ask this question "How are the cell walls of a plant different from that on an animal?" or you can rephrase the same question like so: "What model can you build to identify the difference between a plant and an animal cell?" Perhaps the best way to ask learners to do something is to have them interact with each other in groups or partnerships. The previous question asks learners to do something by adding, "Ask your partner, 'How are the cell walls of a plant different from that on an animal?' and create a T-chart of the differences." When learners have to do something useful with the questions, it increases engagement, especially if all of the learners are expected to perform.

## Learner-Inspired Questions

The most authentic questions will come from the learners themselves. Often the learners' questions percolate to the top after the formal learning, but they are still valid questions and, if not resolved or answered, can get in the way of future learning. That is why it is important to set up a system that encourages learners to share their questions at any time, not just by raising their hands in class. Another reason for creating such a system is that some learners do not want the attention for multiple reasons but feel they can contribute. You know these individuals because they appear to be attentive in class, but, unless called on, they will never volunteer. For face-to-face classes, reserving a spot on the wall for a question parking lot where learners can post their questions, asking learners to give you their questions as an exit ticket as they leave the room, or placing a shoe box on a desk as a question box may be physical ways to get those extra questions. Message boards, questions threads, emails, or third-party message services like Remind may be even more attractive to your learners for sharing their questions. In order to encourage learner questions, it takes more than simply asking the Zombie Question, "Any questions?" It requires that you actually deal with the questions the learners do ask. As a warning, savvy learners in class also know that if they ask the right question, it may trigger your interest and get you off topic to send the whole group down an unnecessary rabbit hole. What I am referring to is that if they put questions on an electronic message board and the instructor never references those questions, they will stop putting them there. Make it a daily habit to check the question gathering system that you created and find a way to incorporate those questions in the lesson for the day.

## Summary

1   The more you know about your audience, the better you can customize questions that will be able to meet their needs and garner interest and engagement.

2   Keep in tune with what is pertinent and relevant to your learners.
3   Allusions save time because you are tapping into common knowledge learners already possess.
4   When learners are asked to do something in a question, they will remember (learn) more. Group and partner work are ideal question activities that help all the learners do something.
5   When questions come from the learner, that automatically raises the interest and engagement level of that particular learner and all the learners.

## Questions to Consider

1   What questions can I create for a particular participant or group of learners in my classroom that take advantage of what I know about them?

_____

_____

_____

2   What current "hot topics" can I incorporate into my questions?

_____

_____

_____

3   What questions from my current course of study can make allusions to things my learners understand?

_____

_____

_____

4   How do I plan adjust my questions from "whole-class" questions to partner and group questions?

_____

_____

_____

5   What system can I create to gather authentic learner questions at any time?

_____

_____

_____

## 8.2  How to Tier Questions by Complexity and Difficulty

The idea of making question more rigorous is to make the questions more challenging cognitively. The only way to do that is to require the learner to use different mental processes that require more brain power. In 1956, Dr. Benjamin Bloom created a taxonomy of the cognitive domain.[4] We have used his taxonomy as the measuring stick[5] for rigor since then, yet we still struggle to get above knowledge and comprehension on the low end of the stick.

The idea of tiering questions is that the initial questions posed by the instructor or other learners are easier and prepare the learner for the harder, more complex questions that come later (see Figure 8.1). In Bloom's Taxonomy, Dr. Bloom starts with knowledge and comprehension and then works his way up to Synthesis (creation, creative thinking, and problem solving) (see Section 3.2). Since 1956, when Bloom's Taxonomy was written, it has become evident that specific question words correlate directly with which level of thinking would be required to answer the questions (see Table 8.1).[6]

Table 8.1  Tiered Levels of Questioning

| *Bloom's Taxonomy Question Word Stems* | | |
| --- | --- | --- |
| **Cognitive Level** | **Trigger Verbs** | **Question Stems** |
| *Knowledge* | list, recite, outline, define, name, quote, recall, identify, label, recognize, choose, describe, define, identify, locate, memorize, recite, recognize, select, state | What . . . ?, Where . . . ?, Who . . . ?, When . . . ?, How many . . . ?, How much? |
| *Comprehension, Understanding* | describe, paraphrase, restate, compare, summarize, contrast, interpret, discuss, demonstrate, distinguish, explain, express, extend, relate, illustrate, indicate, interrelate, interpret, infer, judge, match, paraphrase, represent, restate, rewrite, select, omit, match | What are . . . ? How can you restate . . . ? What is the function of . . . ? What does . . . mean? Is this the same as . . . ? What is the definition of . . . ? State in one word . . . ? How can you explain what is happening in . . . ? What is meant by . . . ? |

**Bloom's Taxonomy Question Word Stems**

| Cognitive Level | Trigger Verbs | Question Stems |
|---|---|---|
| *Application* | calculate, predict, apply, solve, illustrate, use, demonstrate, determine, model, perform, present, apply, choose, dramatize, explain, generalize, judge, organize, paint, prepare, produce, select, show, sketch, solve, use, graph | How ... ? <br> What is an example of ... ? <br> How would you use ... ? <br> What are the steps for ... ? <br> How would you graph ... ? <br> What procedures would you try for ... ? <br> How would you solve the math problem? <br> How would you graph ... ? <br> What expectations are there in ... ? |
| *Analysis* | classify, break down, categorize, analyze, diagram, illustrate, simplify, associate, classify, compare, differentiate, distinguish, identify, interpret, point out, subdivide, survey | Which ... ?, Which one? <br> What's fact? What's opinion? <br> What errors do you see ... ? <br> What assumptions ... ? <br> What inconsistencies do you find ... ? <br> What distinctions exist between ... and ... ? <br> What is the premise of ... ? <br> What's the main idea? <br> What style is used in ... ? <br> What techniques are employed in ... ? <br> What does the graph indicate ... ? |
| *Evaluation, Critical Thinking* | choose, support, relate, determine, defend, judge, grade, compare, prioritize, contrast, argue, justify, support, convince, select, evaluate, appraise, infer, judge, criticize, defend, translate | Why ... ?, <br> Which is the best one? <br> Which is more valuable? <br> What is the most important? <br> How would you prioritize ... ? <br> How can you support your opinion? <br> What conclusions can you make from ... ? <br> What fallacies are evident in ... ? <br> What does the author believe? <br> What is your point of view on ... ? |
| *Synthesis, Creative Thinking, Problem Solving* | design, formulate, build, invent, create, compose, generate, derive, modify, develop, choose, combine, compose, construct, create, design, develop, do, formulate, hypothesize, invent, make, make up, originate, organize, plan, produce, improve, predict | What fallacies/consistencies/ inconsistencies appear? <br> Which is more important/moral/better/ logical/valid/appropriate? <br> Find the errors. <br> Predict what would happen if.... |

Types of knowledge can be tiered along with types of thinking. Erickson's Concept-Based Curriculum (Erickson, Lanning, & French, 2017) relates to complexity of thinking with different types of knowledge.[7] Her progression starts at Facts, then progresses onto Topics, Concepts, Principles, Generalizations, and then Theories. She maintains that the initial aim of learning should be concept level, not the topic or facts levels. Certainly, topics and facts need to be acquired in order to do this, but those should not be the focus. Once the learners arrive at the concept level of knowledge, then they can begin to generalize and transfer understanding to other concepts and principles. I have included Bloom's Taxonomy in Figure 8.1 as well as Costa's Questioning Levels.

My own research indicates that, in terms of the learning perspective, there is a different hierarchy that needs to be used (see Table 8.1). Let me preface my explanation with this statement: you as the instructor do not have to ask all of these questions, learner by learner, until every person in the whole class has answered the question. There is a much easier way to get all participants to answer the questions. One of the most underused pieces of learning equipment is the four walls of the classroom and the hallway outside the classroom. You are able to place visual representations of what knowledge you want the learners to acquire on the four walls and even the floor and ceiling if you want. Then, when you go through the tiered questions or your learners go through the tiered questions with their partners, they can reference what is on the walls in multiple ways. If you wish to lead the learners in tiered questions instead of assigning the questions to groups, I suggest that, for maximum benefit, all the learners be expected to answer the questions at the same time, either verbally (chorally) or with some physical movement. (Section 13.5 talks about Total Physical Response in more depth.)

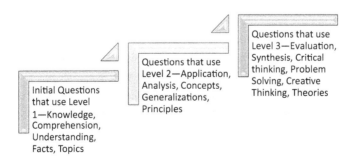

**Figure 8.1** Tiered Levels of Questioning

## Tiered Questions for Knowledge Development

First, the statements of fact need to be provided to induce knowledge or, if using the walls, creating a correlation between what is said and what is seen. I call this first tier "exposure." Once the learners have become sufficiently familiar with the facts, then real learning happens with questions.

First are the simple recognition questions:

◆ Is this a cat?
◆ Is this an endoplasmic reticulum?
◆ Is this a hard drive?
◆ Is this a marketing objective?

Using minimal pairs is a good way to help them recognize the differences and safely begin to use the vocabulary.

◆ Is this a gopher or a groundhog?
◆ Is this a pony or a horse?
◆ Is this a fraction or a percent?
◆ Is this a noun or a pronoun?
◆ Is this a variable or a constant?

Then the next step is to get the learner to produce the label, term, or concept with short-answer questions.

◆ What is this?
◆ What is the scientific name for cat?
◆ What do you call the cord that you attach to your computer?

Then, more difficult still:

◆ What do you use when it is raining?
◆ When it is cold what do you put on?
◆ When you want to end a sentence, what punctuation do you use?
◆ If you want to cash a check, where do you go?
◆ Oxygen combined with hydrogen makes what chemical compound?
◆ What common chemical compound do we use at the table that has chlorine in it?

From there you tier into more cognitively challenging questions. In this level, it is useful to require learners to answer in complete sentences even though the questions could be answered with one or just a few words. You may provide the sentence stems or a sentence stem model in advance.

- ◆ I'm traveling to Europe from Florida; what modes of transportation can I use?
- ◆ I am packing for a journey to Argentina in December; what clothing should I bring?
- ◆ The war of 1812 was between which two nations?
- ◆ When I place a cathode and an anode in water and add electricity, what gasses are released?
- ◆ How can I determine the answer to a problem if I have two variables and two constants?

The most difficult tiers of questions are those of values and opinions. For example:

- ◆ When Shakespeare's Hamlet said "to be, or not to be," what do you think he was talking about?
- ◆ Why would people trust Punxsutawney Phil to predict the length of the winter season?
- ◆ Which is more effective in keeping you warm, a jacket or a sweater?

Table 8.2  Bloom's Action Words and Question Starters

| Table of Question Tiers for the Learning Process | |
| --- | --- |
| 1. Knowledge | Repeated audio and visual exposure to content in context to bring familiarity |
| 2. Recognition | Correlation between what is seen and what is heard—a vocabulary definition, for example |
| 3. Understanding | Prompt to identify a concept verbally, in writing, or physically. |
| 4. Distinction | Prompt to differentiate a concept from a similar one verbally, in writing, or physically |
| 5. Production | Given the meaning or definition, being able to produce the word or concept in context |
| 6. Manipulation | Being able to apply the concept to the correct situations |
| 7. Value | Weighing the relative worth, utility, or effect of the concept personally or in larger contexts |
| 8. Opinion | Personalizing preference or likes regarding the concept |
| 9. Creation | Using knowledge to communicate questions and ideas or form/build/construct new concepts. |

◆ When writing sentences, how do you think that you could use punctuation to exhibit emotion best?

◆ Which war, the War of 1812 or the French Revolution, resulted in more benefits to the common people, in your opinion?

The final portion of the tiered questioning is actually in the learner's control. Now the learner is using the knowledge and asking their own questions (see Section 14.1).

### Section 8.2 Summary

1 Tiered questions progress from simple facts to requesting the learners to create new ideas and theories.

2 Bloom's taxonomy corresponds with action verbs that are used in questions to encourage learners to use that form of thinking.

3 A new model for inspiring learning using tiered questions includes exposure, recognition, understanding, distinction, production, manipulations, value, opinion, and creation.

### Questions to Consider

1 How will I implement a tiered question progression in my current course of study?
Exposure:

_____

_____

_____

Recognition:

_____

_____

_____

Understanding:

_____

_____

_____

Distinction:

_____

_____

_____

Production:

_____

_____

_____

Manipulations:

_____

_____

_____

Value:

_____

_____

_____

Opinion:

_____

_____

_____

Creation:

_____

_____

_____

## 8.3 Leading Questions vs Probing Questions

### Leading Questions

In sales, leading questions are used all the time to bring the client to the conclusion that the sales person wants them to make, i.e. buy my product or service. For example:

"When you test drove this magnificent car and you sat in the luxurious leather seats, how much did that make you want to buy this car?"

Pollsters use leading questions to get the respondent to respond one particular way. Example:

"In the past weeks we have noticed an increase in rioting and vandal- ism. On a scale of one to five how would you rate your government's ability to handle these situations?"

In our schools, we ask leading questions to help the learners behave. Example:

"Our school rules state that when learners do not walk in a straight line, then they will be sent to the principal. When you did not walk in a straight line, did you want to go see the principal?"

These types of leading questions tend to be frowned upon because they are a method of coercion and manipulation. On the other hand, there are some positive uses for leading questions. We can ask leading questions when we are trying to give the learners a helping hand (see Chapter 9 for scaffold- ing questions). For example,

Topic: Density
   "We've talked about the effect of ice EXPANDING when it freezes; what does that tell you about the density of ice?"
   "Sidewalks have expansion spacers inserted into the cement every four feet. What would happen to the sidewalk on a hot day without the spacers?"
   Topic: Law of Exponents
   "When you multiply two by two, that gives you two squared. What do you get when you multiply 'a' times 'a'?"
   "If $a^2$ times $a^3$ is $a^5$ what is $(a+b)^3$ times $(a+b)^4$?"
   Topic: History
   "The Monroe Doctrine was intended to protect the fledgling democracies of Central and South America from European invasion. Why did the US provide military support to Benito Juarez in Mexico?"
   "Robert E. Lee was a southern general whose leadership won sev- eral battles against Ulysses S. Grant in the civil war. At Gettysburg, what was his fatal mistake?"
   Topic: Literature
   "*Jurassic Park* was written by Michael Crichton and recounted the tragic effort to resurrect dinosaurs from ancient DNA samples. What do you think is the message the author wants us to understand?"
   "Science fiction is a genre that takes human situations and inter- actions and places them in a hypothetical future. How is that different from other fiction?"

Topic: Philosophy

"If we accept that humanism declares that the human experience is the most important element. What does that tell you about Bill Nye, a famous humanist?"

"Stoicism refers to the attitude of acceptance of the world and our situation and not worrying about things over which we have no control. In the writings of Teddy Roosevelt, how is this demonstrated?"

Topic: Computers

"An algorithm is a set of sequential actions designed to perform a function and is brought into play by a specific command. What commands initiate the Boolean search?"

"The parameter of 'If–Then' in a program allows a variation of actions depending on data that is inputted. If the 'If–Then' statement is false, what happens to the actions?"

## Probing Questions

In creating WILD HOG Questions, i.e. questions created while planning a lesson, consider adding to the main questions possible follow-up questions that probe for deeper understanding. In anticipating possible misconceptions and misunderstandings, a probing question can not only provide the instructor with a general understanding of what the learner knows or thinks, but it can help the learner clarify thinking and start thoughts down more productive veins of inquiry. One nice thing about probing questions is that they are all divergent and open-ended questions, and they are short because the antecedents have already been presented. Here are some examples:

"Can you explain more?"
"When you said . . . what did you mean?"
"What do you understand from . . . ?"
"Can you provide an example?"
"What evidence supports your thoughts?"
"What do you think is most important about . . . ?"
"How does that relate to . . . ?"
"What message do you infer?"
"How did you arrive at . . . ?"

## Summary

1   In most circumstances, leading questions are frowned upon, but examples can be found nearly everywhere, in business, sales, surveys, and the media. The intent for a leading question is to try to guide a person to a particular choice or point of view. In education, leading questions can

facilitate learner success by providing hints, clues, and reminders to help the learner answer or approach the question correctly.

2  Probing questions are used to follow up answers that do not entirely show the learner's thinking or understanding. These questions are open-ended and divergent.

### Questions to Consider

1  In my current course of study, I can write the following leading questions and corollary probing questions in order to help struggling learners:

_____

_____

_____

_____

_____

_____

_____

_____

_____

_____

_____

_____

## 8.4 Coaching and Clarifying With Questions

### Coaching

If we truly believe that learners should be responsible for their own learning, then we must have a "coaching" mindset. We can all envision the idea of athletic coaching; the coach is on the sidelines, and the players are on the field or court showing what they can do. But even some coaches don't get "coaching." You've seen them: the ones that are shouting at their players, screaming commands, and even berating their players for the whole world to see. There are so many things wrong with this, on so many levels. If these coaches exhibit this kind of behavior in front of the fans, they are most likely worse at practice. What a hostile learning environment! The worst problem is the attitude of this type of coach toward their players. Their behavior says:

You need me because I know everything. You need me because I gave you the chance to be here. You have to listen to what I say in order to win. I don't trust you to work things out on your own.

These coaches don't last long, and their teams implode quickly. Unfortunately, I have witnessed this same type of behavior in classrooms from instructors when their questions become interrogations, are sarcastic, or even are ridiculing.

On a better note, we also see the coaches on the other end of the scale. These types are calm, interested, and engaged, but they trust their players to do what had already been decided and practiced. These coaches will call a time-out, but instead of making commands, they ask questions, they point out observations and ask "How are you going to fix it?" These coaches understand that it's not their game; it's the players' game. They understand that there is nothing that the coach can do to force the players to perform and that the most they can do is encourage, inspire, and motivate. Fortunately, I have seen educators like these good coaches who use questions as powerful tools to build trust, self-confidence, and self-worth.

The underlying premise of educational "coaching" is that the coach (the instructor) is not the one doing the work. The coach makes no decisions, goals, or plans for the learner. The coach is not even an advisor. The coach is not the one responsible for learning. The coach, in all interactions with the learner, treats the learner as having sole responsibility for learning. Sole responsibility means that what is learned—or not—is 100% a result of what the learner did or did not accomplish. A true educational coach is nothing more than a positive force acting as a magnifying glass for the learner to view and reflect on behaviors and consequences and always asking "How are you going to make it better?" This is the basis of the "coaching"—and I would say "teaching"—mindset.

## Positive Regard

A coach's finest tools in lighting the fire for learning are questions. All questions that a coach poses to learners should have as their foundation a sincere positive regard for the learner. The best form of positive regard is trust. Trust them to do what they say they were going to do, trust them to be independent thinkers, trust them to be able to figure things out. Trust them to be good learners. Many instructors will say "I'm asking questions because I care," but their questions are more like an interrogation, which makes the learner feel on the offensive or embarrassed or ashamed. If an educational coach (instructor) really cares, then a simple mental switch is all it takes to ask questions showing not only that you really do care and trust the learner but also that you hold them in high regard.

Any question that begins with "Did you . . . ?" automatically assumes that they "didn't." The same can be said with questions that begin with "Didn't you," "Why didn't you," and "Why . . . ?" In response to these types of questions, the learner is put on the offensive, having to justify action or nonaction. It doesn't matter the tone of the question, or the way you ask them, the result is the same. I think of Professor Dolores Umbridge, from the *Harry Potter* series, who would ask the most horrible questions in the sweetest possible voice, which actually made the question worse. Flipping the manner in which we ask the question can transform an accusatorial tone (regardless of how sweetly we say it) to a tone of trust and confidence. This is how we flip the question: we assume that whatever the point of the question is, that the learner has already done it and we want to know the result. How does that work? If we are tempted to say, "Did you multiply both sides of the equation by a factor of two?" if the learner has done so, he may think, "I'm not an idiot! Give me a break!" or if he has not done so, he may think, "No, I didn't, yet. You think I'm stupid and you have to show me everything!" Either way, the learner gets a negative message from a seemingly innocuous question. Changing a few words in the same question by assuming the task has been done and then asking about the result has the opposite effect. "What was the result when you multiplied both sides by a factor of two?" If this had been done already, the learner would most likely appreciate that you gave him credit for it. It becomes an affirmation. If he had not done it, the learner would feel pleased that you at least thought he had done it and would have no

**Table 8.3** How to Tier Questions to Match Learning Process

**Turning Questions From Negative to Positive**

| Negative Nagging | Presuming Positive Intent |
|---|---|
| - Why haven't you studied your words? You had plenty of time. | + *Tell me what you did with your time yesterday.* |
| - Did you remember to do your homework? | + *When you did your homework, what did you find most difficult?* |
| - Did you factor the polynomial first? | + *What steps did you take to solve this problem?* |
| - Did you study your vocabulary for tomorrow's test? | + *How did you prepare for your vocabulary test tomorrow?* |
| - Why didn't you answer the questions? | + *Please explain how you answered the questions.* |
| - Why did you get the wrong answer? | + *How did you arrive at this conclusion?* |
| - Can't you see why this won't work? | +*When you analyzed this problem, what did you discover?* |

qualms about saying, "That's a great idea, I have not done that yet." Table 8.3 gives some examples on how to change interrogations into affirmations.

## Being the Magnifying Glass

An effective coach simply has to be observant enough to be able to shine a light on a problem and explain what they see in such a way that it allows the learner to also see clearly, like looking through a magnifying glass. An elementary teacher might say, "I noticed that your usually high quality of work is starting to drop. What do you think are the reasons for this?" A college professor might say this, "You mentioned to me before that you struggle with statistics. What is your plan to enhance your capacity to analyze statistically?" A high school math teacher may say, "You took the time to write each step you took carefully. What could you do to make sure that each step you took is accurate?" A trainer of trainers for English language proficiency may ask the group, "I see that most of you rated this writing sample as a 1. Talk with your elbow partner and discuss why you did not rate it as a 2 or a 3."

## The Fallacy of Positive Criticism

Another aspect of coaching questions I want to clarify is the overused idea of positive criticism. When we want to say, "I'm telling this to you for your own good," it may not be for a learner's good, but it makes us feel like we have done some sort of duty. In a learning situation, be it classroom, online, or workshop conference room, when we ask questions "for their own good," to show the learners how much they have yet to learn, we are really showing them how smart we are by demeaning them. Ostensibly some professors, instructors, and teachers like to use questions Socratically, to point out flaws in a learners' thinking, "Class, what errors can you see in her answer?" Assuming positive intent, the better question would be, "Class, her answer has merit. Who could help her strengthen her position?" I am not saying that errors should not be corrected, just that there is nothing positive about doing it in front of the whole class. Let's say the answer given by the learner was completely off-base; acknowledge the effort at least,

> Thank you for being willing to answer that very difficult question and that is the first step in getting an answer that may work. Would it be alright if I gave you some time to think about it, and I'll come back to you?

Socrates would even agree that, for learning's sake, just giving the "right" answer would be a mistake. If a learner has to think about something, then the memory of that thing will be enhanced. Helping the learner figure out their own mistakes reinforces the concept that the learner is really in charge of their own learning. If we really feel that a learner could benefit from some piece of wisdom that we have, then, as an effective coach, we will ask perhaps the most powerful question because it gives power to the learner: "Would you like some advice?"

## Summary

1   Just as an athletic coach has to allow the players to take full responsibility for their performance, educational coaches (instructors) must change the mindset of the learners to believe the same.

2   The most important tool an instructor has is the relationship with the learner. Too often this relationship is adversarial. With positive regard, the learner is empowered and feels that the instructor is there to help, not judge.

3   The purpose for the educational coach is to help the learners clearly see the target and their mistakes so that the learners can fix them and do better the next time.

4   Positive criticism is really not positive. Helping a participant to see their own mistake is a better way to correct errors. Asking the participant if they would like help or advice is another better way of fixing misconceptions and errors.

## Questions to Consider

1   How can I adopt a coaching viewpoint in my instruction?

_____

_____

_____

2   In my current studies, I can show positive regard in the following questions:

_____

_____

_____

_____

_____

_____

_____

_____

_____

_____

## 8.5  How to Extend Understanding With Questions

### How to Push Participants to Dig Deeper

In my book, *Teaching Students to Dig Deeper*,[8] I emphasize that questioning should be used to engage all learners, whether that means that all participants answer a question out loud at the same time, or that the question will be answered with a partner given a one-minute time frame, or that learners will all move their bodies in some way to answer the question (see Chapter 12). All participants must be engaged for the question to be effective. I am sorry to say that that eliminates the traditional instructor-led discussion, which is never really a discussion with the entire class—usually, it is just a discussion with few uninhibited participants (see Chapter 13). The point is to get all learners to a deeper level of thinking using powerful questions, and don't forget that the learner is the one digging, not the instructor. We have talked about tiered questioning in Section 8.2, i.e. starting out with knowledge recognition questions and gradually increasing the difficulty and complexity. Here, we are assuming the knowledge and comprehension has been acquired.

In doing the research for my book, *Teaching Students to Dig Deeper*, I discovered ten college- and career- readiness traits that all individuals need in order to be successful in both, as well as life. These are listed in Figure 8.2.

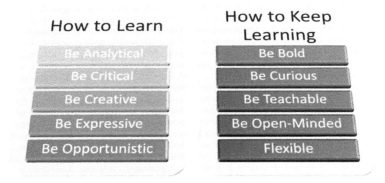

Figure 8.2  Ten Essential Skills for College- and Career- Readiness

Table 8.4 Questions Correlated to the Ten Essential Skills for College- and Career- Readiness

**Questions to Inspire Learners**

| Digging Deeper Traits | Example Questions |
|---|---|
| Be Analytical | How does it work?<br>What steps did you take?<br>What is missing?<br>What are the rules? |
| Be Critical | Which is the best option? Why?<br>What value does this have?<br>What is your opinion? Why?<br>Why does or doesn't it work? |
| Be Creative | How do you improve this?<br>What else could you do?<br>How would you solve this?<br>What would you create if . . . ? |
| Be Expressive | How do you feel about . . . ?<br>What are your thoughts?<br>How do you explain your thinking?<br>What could you do to persuade me? |
| Be Opportunistic | What do you propose?<br>What else can you learn?<br>What options do you have?<br>What can you do right now? |
| Be Bold | What should you do?<br>How would you find out?<br>What obstacles do you see?<br>What advantages are there? |
| Be Curious | What do you see?<br>What do you notice that is unique?<br>What interests you most?<br>What if I changed one thing . . . ? |
| Be Teachable | Where could you get the answers?<br>What does the research say?<br>How could you tell if it is correct?<br>Who could answer your questions? |
| Be Open-Minded | What other viewpoints are there?<br>What is the opposite view?<br>How do you reconcile your thoughts with others?<br>What is your plan if you are wrong? |
| Be Flexible | What is your plan B?<br>What variables do you have to consider?<br>What clarification do you need?<br>How do you adjust for changes? |

In Chapter 6, we looked at designing WILD HOG Questions that were rigorous and how to create a question progression. Rather than give you the full explanations for each of these characteristics, which is what I did in *Teaching Students to Dig Deeper*, since this book is solely about questions, I will give you some ideas about how to ask questions that promote these characteristics for deeper digging in your learners (see Table 8.4).

## Extension Questions

Similar to the probing questions discussed in Section 8.3, extension questions push a learner to expand thinking and to take intellectual forays into the unexplored territory. These questions, as with all others, should be WILD HOG companions and written before instruction. These questions dwell in the Level 3, Synthesis (creation, problem solving), and Theory levels of rigor discussed in Chapter 6. At this level of questioning, I suggest that you also ask your learners, teams, groups, partnerships, etc. to reflect on what they have learned and how to improve learning. As with all questions, all learners must do something with the question. I envision groups or partners hashing out the answers to these deep questions. Here are some examples:

"What if you could change one thing?"
"How would you end the story?"
"What will the future look like without . . . ?"
"How would you make a better . . . ?"
"What if you could go back in time . . . ?"
"How could you find out more . . . ?"
"What else is there to discover . . . ?"
"What were your successes?"
"What would you like to investigate further . . . ?"
"What did you learn from this . . . ?"
"How could you improve your performance in . . . ?"
"What advice would you give to your team or those who follow you?"

## Summary

1   The ten college- and career- readiness traits can be divided into two parts: skills needed to learn and skills to keep learning.
2   Extending learning happens once the basics are completed, and, with "what if" and reflection questions, learners will be able to deepen their understanding.

## Questions to Consider

1 I plan to use the following questions to deepen learning in my current instruction.

_____

_____

_____

_____

_____

_____

_____

_____

_____

_____

_____

_____

_____

_____

_____

_____

_____

_____

_____

# 8.6 Culturally Sensitive Questions

## Allowing for Culture

The multicultural mania pervasive in today's society insists that everything must take into account and must fully embrace other cultures. I am not sure that that is possible with every question we ask or the manner in which the question is asked. As an instructor, there are few of us who could ask the questions in every language represented in our conference halls, workshops, and classrooms. Being sensitive and making allowances for other cultures does not mean we have to leave ours at the door when we enter the room. What it does mean is that if you have certain procedures or operations that other cultures might misinterpret, explain what you are doing and why. For example, in my Spanish classes, as I asked questions, I expected the male learners to be gentlemen and the female learners to be ladies, I took the time to explain what that meant and how they should respond to my questions. In other cultures, the expectations of male and female may be different. In regard to different languages, as will be discussed in Section 8.7, comprehension is the key in any language, which makes the instructor's job much easier—just make sure to have multiple comprehension clues and cues for every question. The only way to adjust your questions to account for cultural differences is to get to know your audience beforehand. After that, take into account their background knowledge to restrict allusions to things with which they have experience; snow, foods, movies, history, etc. My experience is that people are more alike than they are different. The other advice I offer is to not worry about how some participants respond to your questions. For example, some cultures view it as offensive if they look you in the eyes.[9]

## Avoiding Cultural Assumptions

My wife and I had a yard sale and had a number of people interested buying our stuff. One couple looked Hispanic, and, since I speak Spanish, I spoke to them in Spanish. They just looked at me strangely and did not answer. They were obviously offended, but were polite about it. I reverted to English and apologized for speaking to them in Spanish. They explained that they were Navajo and did not speak Spanish. I learned the lesson that I should stop making assumptions about cultures. I believe that we should make cultural allowances and that doing so is not cultural appropriation. If using Spanish vocabulary will help a native Hispanic learner understand a question, then I will use it, making sure that I know the meaning of the words first.

## Identifying Your Biases

An interesting professional development activity for the instructor who is sincerely intent on being culturally sensitive is to invite an observer into your instructional space and have the observer track your interactions according to gender and race. A simple grid can show the placement of the learners in the group, and with an easy-to-remember shorthand the observer can put simply write "IQ" for instructor question, "PQ" for participant questions, and thatch marks for repetitions. Another eye-opening activity is having your lesson video-recorded and then reviewing that video with someone whom you trust. Watching it by yourself makes it too easy to ignore uncomfortable truths, and an observer will keep you honest. Each of us has biases or preferences that we don't think we have, and these are good ways to discover them. More will be discussed about this topic in section 8.7.

## Summary

1   Being culturally sensitive requires flexibility and patience, but it does not require that you get rid of your own culture. With explanations and adjustments, your culture and others in the group can coexist. Often language is a barrier, and trying to communicate in other languages for comprehension's sake is appropriate. Be careful about allusions to things that are culturally specific, which others might not know about.
2   Avoiding cultural assumptions is as easy as getting to know your audience. Just ask them.
3   Either video-record yourself or ask an observer into your lesson to observe and record your instructional behaviors.

### Questions to Consider

1   What efforts will I make to be culturally sensitive in my current instructional situation?

_____

_____

_____

2   What will I have to explain about my questioning process as it relates to culture?

_____

_____

_____

3   How will I check for my personal instructional biases?

_____

_____

_____

## 8.7  Accommodating for Language Learners

When I was in district leadership in a small school district, they had at least a twenty-percent point gap in their testing scores between Anglo learners and Hispanic learners. I knew that the teachers did not teach the Anglo learners any differently than the Hispanic learners. In my investigation, what we discovered were two contributors to the problem. The first was the teacher use of "academic language,"[10] and the second was the learner "lack of background knowledge."[11] Both of these could be related to race, economic status, or culture, but, at the same time, both of these are things the instructors can actually do something about to minimize their effect. Another interesting thing is that accommodating for lack of background knowledge or poor knowledge of academic language has no downsides. It helps all learners understand better.

## English Language Learners

In any learning situation, the participants will have a wide range of language skills, but the job of the instructor is to be able to reach all of them. Asking questions that all learners can comprehend at the same level is a challenge. As I mentioned earlier, overcoming this challenge helps all learners, not just the ones who struggle with English. As the rise in English language learners has increased, so has the need to accommodate for their need to comprehend. Programs such as Sheltered Instruction Method, Communicative Approach, Specially Designed Academic Instruction in English (SDAIE in California), Sheltered Instruction Observation Protocol (SIOP) and English Language Proficiency Standards (ELPS) (in Texas)[12] all are based on the idea that, in order for individuals' learning English to be successful, they must be equipped to understand the question. There are two ways to do this: provide multiple forms of input that relate and access common cultural knowledge and experience, or talk to them in their native tongue. Since I have trouble putting two words together in Mandarin Chinese, I usually opt for the first.

## Comprehensible Input in Questions

Having experience in learning languages and teaching them, I know that comprehension is the key.[13] How do you aid comprehension when you ask questions? Remember that if you do traditional whole-group questions, you are wasting your time and that of the participants, so, when all the participants understand the question, all participants should answer the question. As mentioned earlier, you have to provide multiple sources of input that all point to the understanding you want. According to the SIOP protocol, comprehensible input includes combinations of these visual cues, such as providing:

◆ A picture, diagram, map, or drawing
◆ Video, music, sounds,
◆ Mime, gestures, hand signals, mimicking, pointing,
◆ Dancing, movement,
◆ The actual written question.

As an example, when I taught Spanish, I learned that associating a visual image (I created masterful stick-figure drawings) with the vocabulary that I placed on the walls made comprehensible input come to life. I taught the learners how to respond to vocabulary questions by pointing, touching, or standing beneath the correct vocabulary term. These "recognition" exercises helped the learners to instantly know what the word meant because they could see the picture, and, through repetition, they associated the picture and the concept with the Spanish word. I have found that providing a visual, whether in a PowerPoint lecture or an online presentation, is crucial for making learning easier. This holds true for any age group.

Online learning is all visual, but adding a picture with the words in the question makes understanding and remembering (learning) easier and more enjoyable. Personally, I use photos when available—clipart becomes irritating quickly, so I use it sparingly. In a classroom or presentation room, don't forget the four walls. Placing concept maps,[14] anchor charts,[15] or diagrams on the walls invokes a situational type of memory called Locale memory (see Chapter 3), especially if you invite them to move about physically (see Section 13.5). When you refer to an anchor chart (which includes key points and a visual reminder of knowledge that has been learned), use a pointer or a laser pointer to identify the part that relates to the questions you are going to ask. Then when all the learners respond with the answer, those learning English can see and hear the answer.

## How Do You Build Background Knowledge to Ask Questions?

According to Robert Marzano, building background knowledge can be done in several ways: field trips, virtual field trips, videos, story-telling, and, amazingly . . . reading. The idea is that, in some way, the learner must have an experience, and with that they will be able to associate the new learning with that experience or background knowledge. Other than actual field trips and virtual field trips, video segments are the best way to build background knowledge. An innovative English curriculum produced by The College Board, called SpringBoard, uses short video segments from popular movies to connect learners with literature and writing.[16] US copyright law states that, for educational purposes, instructors may show segments without copyright infringement as long as they can prove it was for educational purposes, not just to fill time.[17] With today's technology, it is a simple thing to clip five minutes or less and put it in a PowerPoint or a learning management system. Short video segments are perfect for setting the stage for all learners to answer and ask questions. To continue high comprehension, when asking questions, use a still image from the video and paste it next to the question.[18]

One thing that helps all learners—but especially learners not fully proficient in English—is sentence starters or sentence stems. Often the learner might know the answer but might not know how to frame it in a sentence. To help these learners, in a partner "ask and answer" session the questions should have a visual and the answer stem.

For example:

If in Australia they wear jackets and gloves, what season of the year is it
   in the month of July?
In Australia, the season for July is_____.

## Summary
1   English language learners and even English-speaking populations within our learning communities have different levels of fluency in "academic" language and often have limited background knowledge.
2   Comprehension can be aided by including contextual clues such as visuals, gestures, writing, drawings, music, and motions.
3   Building background knowledge for learners is essential before you ask questions, and, besides taking them on field trips, video segments and literature are ways to do it. When asking questions, provide a visual stimulus with the written and verbal question, and, to help them answer, provide a sentence stem.

## Questions to Consider
1   What will I do to make sure that I provide the appropriate vocabulary and background knowledge before asking questions?

_____

_____

_____

2   How can I use the four walls of the room to help provide comprehensible input?

_____

_____

_____

3   What questions will I prepare that coincide with my current assignment for which I could provide visual cues and a sentence stem to help?

_____

_____

_____

Question visual cue

_____

_____

_____

Question

_____

_____

_____

Question stem

_____

_____

_____

Question visual cue

_____

_____

_____

Question

_____

_____

_____

Question stem

_____

_____

_____

_____

_____

Question visual cue

_____

_____

_____

Question

_____

_____

_____

Question stem

_____

_____

_____

## Notes

1   See what I did? I alluded to math to talk about history. If you knew that the Pythagorean Theorem deals with triangles then you got the allusion. The theorem describes the relationship of the length of the three sides of a triangle to each other. The formula is $a^2 + b^2 = c^2$.

2   Here is the clip of the flying monkey reference if you want to refresh your memory: https://youtu.be/YnjXScL6G3A. Nick Fury (Samuel L. Jackson) used it to indicate that two men, Hawkeye (Jeremy Renner) and Selvig the scientist (Stellan Skarsgård) were turned into obedient drones by Loki (Tom Hiddleston). It works for Captain America (Chris Evans) because _The Wizard of Oz_ came out in 1939, and he was frozen in ice four years after that, so he knows that allusion. And if you haven't seen _The Wizard of Oz_, then here is a clip about the Wicked Witch of the West's obedient minions, the flying monkeys https://youtu.be/SESI19h4wDo. Both are good flicks—I highly recommend them.

3   This is a clip from the movie Mary Poppins sung by Julie Andrews called "Feed the Birds" https://youtu.be/XHrRxQVUFN4. The point of the song is that some things are more important than a few coins, or tuppences. What is a tuppence? At the time it was 1/120th of a pound sterling, or about a dollar in today's money . . . this was before England went decimal.

4   Benjamin S. Bloom created his Taxonomy of the Cognitive Domain in 1956 when he worked at the University of Chicago. He and his team wrote _Taxonomy of Educational Objectives, Handbook I: The Cognitive Domain_ (1956). The book talks about the psychomotor domain (movement) and the affective domain (emotions), but the only one that really has been used is the Taxonomy of the Cognitive Domain. He proposed that each cognitive activity was a magnitude of difficulty more rigorous than the activity preceding it. His original taxonomy had Evaluation as the most difficult. Since then, his taxonomy has been modified by Lorin Anderson, a former

student of Dr. Bloom, and rightly so, to have synthesis on top see (www.effectiveteaching.com/userfiles/cms/unitFiles/29/GoBe235BloomsTaxonomy.pdf)

5 This allusion refers to more than a yardstick. After graduating from college, there were no teaching jobs available mid-year, so I substituted during the day and worked at a Quickmart convenience store at night. One of my duties was to go outside each night and take a recording of the level of the underground gas tanks. This was Arizona, so it was not so cold mid-winter. I would take a twelve-foot long, square-sided stick that had graduated markings along its length on each side, and, after taking off the metal lid, I would plunge the stick into the tank. With a flashlight, I would read the level of the stick in feet and record it.

6 There are hundreds of lists of Bloom's Taxonomy trigger words. Here are just a few: https://bloomstaxonomy.net, https://coe.uni.edu/sites/default/files/wysiwyg/BloomRevisedTaxonomy.pdf, https://tips.uark.edu/using-blooms-taxonomy/

7 H. Lyn Erickson is the "godmother" of concept-based curriculum. The idea that concept knowledge transfers but not factual knowledge is foundational to her theories. If learners understand one concept, they can transfer that knowledge or generalize it to other situations. Erickson, H. L.; Lanning, L. A.; & French, R. (2017). *Concept-based curriculum and instruction for the thinking classroom second edition*. Corwin a SAGE Publishing Company. ISBN 9781506355399. See her Structure of Knowledge illustration here in Chapter 1 of Tools for Teaching Conceptual Understanding: https://us.corwin.com/sites/default/files/upm-binaries/82739_Chapter_1___Tools_for_Teaching_Conceptual_Understanding%2C_Secondary.pdf

8 My first book, *Teaching Students to Dig Deeper: The Common Core in Action*, was published in 2012, and the second edition was published in 2017: *Teaching Students to Dig Deeper: Ten Essential Skills for College and Career Readiness*. Both published by Eye on Education through Routledge.

9 It's not a classroom myth reported over decades. Read more in this article about cultures and eye contact: www.brighthubeducation.com/social-studies-help/9626-learning-about-eye-contact-in-other-cultures/

10 These researchers compared the idea of understanding academic language and reading comprehension and found out they have many things in common, but the most surprising thing was that the key to improving both was simple: vocabulary development. Kim, Y. G., Petscher, Y., Uccelli, P., & Kelcey, B. (2020)

11 Robert Marzano wrote an answer to the lack of background knowledge in his book *Building Background Knowledge* (2004). In it he describes the

struggles of students in trying to understand allusions and references to things with which they have no experience.

12  For more information on SIOP instructional tools for English language learners, see https://cal.org/siop/ and www.researchgate.net/publication/234632113_The_Sheltered_Instruction_Observation_Protocol_A_Tool_for_Teacher-Research_Collaboration_and_Professional_Development_Educational_Practice_Report_3

13  John DeMado, a language learning advocate, stresses that, if there is no comprehensible input for the learner, we are wasting our time. Learn about John here: https://fluency.consulting/2020/12/03/introducing-john-demado/ and his consulting company here: www.demado-seminars.com/curriculum.htm

14  There are all sorts of concept maps: bubble, hierarchical, mind maps, etc. For example: https://litemind.com/what-is-mind-mapping/

15  Information about anchor charts: first off, it helps if the students are the ones who created the chart. Here is a link that will help: www.weareteachers.com/anchor-charts-101-why-and-how-to-use-them-plus-100s-of-ideas/

16  SpringBoard® from The CollegeBoard® provides math and ELA curriculum for grades 6–12. Since it is a different way for the students to learn, The CollegeBoard® provide considerable teacher training and resources. https://springboard.collegeboard.org/ela/features

17  Here is a succinct copyright explanation for teachers: www.edutopia.org/copyright-rules-teachers

18  The Cambridge University Press and Smart Technologies put together a free-access repository of royalty-free media and software for schools to use. https://gg4l.com/

## References

Stevenson, R. (1964). *Mary Poppins*. Anaheim, CA: Walt Disney Studios Motion Pictures.

Whedon, J. (2012). *The Avengers*. Burbank, CA: Marvel Studios/Walt Disney Studios Motion Pictures.

Bloom, B. S. (1956). *Taxonomy of educational objectives, handbook I: The cognitive domain*. New York: David McKay Co Inc.

Erickson, H. L., Lanning, L. A., & French, R. (2017). *Concept-based curriculum and instruction for the thinking classroom* (2nd ed.). Corwin a SAGE Publishing Company. ISBN 9781506355399

Johnson, B. (2017). *Teaching students to dig deeper: Ten essential skills for college and career readiness*. New York: Routledge.

Kim, Y.-S. G., Petscher, Y., Uccelli, P., & Kelcey, B. (2020). Academic language and listening comprehension—Two sides of the same coin? An empirical examination of their dimensionality, relations to reading comprehension, and assessment modality. *Journal of Educational Psychology, 112*(7), 1367–1387. https://doi.org/10.1037/edu0000430

Marzano, R. (2004). *Building background knowledge for academic achievement.* Alexandria, VA: Association for Supervision and Curriculum Development

# 9

# How to Scaffold Questions

## How Does Scaffolding Questions Build on Participant Success?

Scaffolding a building allows brick layers to safely add rows of bricks to a building. In the same way, scaffolding questions is a way to build on knowledge by asking questions meant to connect and build on previous knowledge. The purpose of scaffolding questions is to systematically prepare the learner to be successful in answering them. As you will learn in Chapter 13, high-level scaffolding questions are difficult to create while you are teaching. To create great scaffolding questions, the first thing to do is to think of the things that learners might find difficult, like allusions to literature they may not have read or to history they of which they may be unaware.[1] Then while you write your plan for instruction, design the WILD HOG scaffolding questions to meet the needs of particular learners (audience). Instructors should be proficient at scaffolding questions or, in other words, helping learners be successful in answering questions, according to difficulty and complexity using Bloom's, Costa's, and Erickson's theories (see Chapter 6).

## 9.1  What Does a Scaffolding Question Look Like?

There are two ways to scaffold questions.

1) Provide verbal explanations and visual cues of the terms or references within the question, with which the learner may not be familiar. I'm not suggesting you be so pedantic as to ask the questions, "What

color was George Washington's white horse?", but a better question would be "What caused George Washington, our first president of the United States, to say 'I cannot tell a lie'?" Perhaps a less-contrived example might be, "The discovery of North America by Christopher Columbus, in 1492, led to an age of European exploration. Who sponsored Columbus' voyage?"

2) The second way to scaffold questions is to prime the pump before asking the questions. Remind the learners of what you have studied, and visually and verbally provide the history, reference, or knowledge that they need prior to asking questions about it. Briefly telling the story about George Washington cutting down the cherry tree or showing on a map from where Christopher Columbus departed on his journey will help all learners remember (learn). For online learning and ancient technological history (35 years ago), the idea of "hyper" learning was developed in order to provide a definition or explanation when the user clicked on a colored word. Today, we can send participants to whole websites and videos in the same way. Helping participants learning English with a mini lesson prior to asking questions scaffolds the learning so that they can incrementally build on what they already know.

Scaffolding questions, just like all questions, are series questions that start with low-level questions, then move on to higher level questions. You wouldn't have your learners ask each other "What clothes do you wear in July in Australia?" before they ask, "Since Australia is south of the equator, are the seasons the same as in the United States, or are they opposite?" Learners cannot ask too many questions. Recycling the questions in different ways is another way of scaffolding because they have seen the question before, and they will recognize a different form of the question as it is repeated. Another way to help scaffold questions is in the answer process. If the learners get the question wrong, they can put the question in the "swing back and let me answer it again" pile, or they can choose a "lifeline" as in the television game show *Who Wants to Be a Millionaire?*

## Summary

1 Scaffolding is a way to make sure that the learners are successful in answering the questions. It includes considering your audience and their learning needs and making adjustments as you prepare your WILD HOG Questions with the lesson.

2 There are two ways to scaffold questions. The first is to include unknown or forgotten information in the question itself. The second way is to teach

a mini lesson before asking the questions. In both ways, you are priming the pump so the learners will know enough to answer the questions effectively.

## Note

1   We cannot assume that learners born after 2001, for example, would know much about or appreciate September 11th or, even less, references to rotary phones, videotapes, cassettes, or typewriters.

### Questions to Consider

1   What kind of preparation do I need to do to create scaffolded questions for my current learners?

_____

_____

_____

2   Here are some examples of my scaffolding question progressions from Level 1 to Level 3:

_____

_____

_____

Level 1

_____

_____

_____

Level 2

_____

_____

_____

Level 3

_____

_____

_____

3    What advanced preparation will I have to do to prepare the learners to be successful in answering the questions?

_____

_____

_____

_____

_____

_____

# 10

# Knowledge and Comprehension Questions

## How Can Questions Prepare Participants to Learn?

In the previous chapter on scaffolding questions, we looked at the incremental nature of scaffolding. The first scaffolding questions are knowledge-based, then move to comprehension of that knowledge. There is nothing more important than knowledge and comprehension. We can't go any further in learning without those two things. The Common Core identifies this knowledge as foundational knowledge.[1] The travesty in many learning scenarios is that they do not go past knowledge and comprehension into the application and previously mentioned categories (see Section 3.2 and Chapter 6).

The acquisition of knowledge and comprehension (including recognition) is solidly based in behavioral psychology and the Taxon memory system: stimulus–response–repetition–association process. With knowledge and comprehension, memory (learning) is obtained by the repetitive association of a concept with words, symbols, or other concepts. Just as stated in Chapter 8, comprehensible input is the key to learning (memory). Most of the learning regarding knowledge and comprehension is vocabulary development, which understandably is like learning a foreign language. Also, as described in Chapter 8, we cannot assume that our "academic language" is understood in the same way by all learners, so we must take steps to train the learners in the vocabulary. I used the word "train" because these vocabulary words and concepts should be like sight words; when they see them, they immediately know what it means.[2]

## 10.1  Taxon Memory Questions

To develop vocabulary,–or knowledge and comprehension–you use the Taxon memory system discussed in section 3.2, which depends on repetition to get the information to stick in learners' brains. Once is not enough, nor is telling your learners to memorize it. The instructor must give multiple opportunities to the learners to recall the targeted information through effective questioning (Rule of Three). These questions will be Level 1 on Costa's questioning Levels. "What is . . . ? Who is . . . ? When did . . . ? What are . . . ? How many . . . ?" are examples of Level 1 questions. These questions are closed and convergent, meaning there is only one answer.

## 10.2  Flash Card Questions

One good way to get all the learners involved and to push the short-term memory into long-term memory is using flashcards with the term on one side and the definition on the other. For example, a question, "What does meiosis mean?", would correspond with what is written on the other side as the answer, "It means cell division by splitting in two parts containing half the DNA." The flash-card methodology can be done online, with partners, small groups, and even the whole group. It can be done without flashcards also; just a list of questions and answers is sufficient. Often a visual image or gesture (non-verbal representation as discussed in Section 8.7) can accompany the words to assure comprehension for all learners and especially language learners.

When I was a Spanish teacher, we had volumes of vocabulary to learn. To get all the learners involved and to help them get to the recognition stage, I made flashcards and had my learners form two lines, A and B, facing each other. Line A had the flashcards; line B rotated. Each learner in row A with the flashcards was the expert and helped their partner learner in row B to master the word or phrase on the card. They had 15 seconds to master the word, then they moved left to the next flashcard. Once all the way through the line three times, the two lines switched roles, and row A now went through the line three times. In this manner, all learners could go through the line three times and master the content of the flashcards in a five-minute rush. Since my Spanish classes were conversational, I used this same process to get learners to ask and answer full questions in Spanish. Another activity in which the learners are asking the low-level questions is to have the questions preprinted for one half of the group and the answers for the other half, and the task is to ask your question until you find the person who has the answer. That person becomes your partner for the next round of questions.

Rarely do they know how to memorize, and few instructors take the time to show them. The same can be said of flash-card questions. In using the flash-card method with partners and small groups, I need to point out that speed is essential. Since the brain works at the speed of light (see Section 2.7), going slow is a waste of time. Teach the learners that, as they quickly go through the flash-cards, if the learners do not know the answer immediately, they need to look at the answer and then put that card in the "review again" pile. This process is repeated until the "review again" pile disappears. To effectively use this process, especially with younger learners, the instructor might need to do "popcorn-style"[3] questions with small groups until they can do it on their own.

## 10.3  Rule of Three

As with all learning, we cannot expect learners to get it right after just one repetition. That is why I taught my learners about the Rule of Three, which demands that things be done at least three times before they start learning or remembering (see the next chapter for more details). They needed to know that doing something just once wasn't going to build muscle memory, recall, or habits of mind. This was a lifesaver for me because it took the burden of learning off of my shoulders and put it on the shoulders of the learners. To complaints of "I don't know!" I was able to respond, "How many times minimum does it take to know?". "Yeah, yeah, at least three." I didn't have to hound my learners, well, some of them I did, but most knew that "practice" meant at least doing it three times.

The Rule of Three applies to the instructor as well. The flash-card method would be one iteration of the Rule of Three to help the learners capture knowledge and understand it. Another iteration could be that the learners create a frequently asked question book or webpage using the knowledge already garnered. A final iteration could be that the learners create a mind-map or anchor chart of the questions and concepts learned. Having done this, they will be ready to put their knowledge to work in higher-level learning such as application,

### Summary

1   Knowledge and comprehension questions are the foundation for learning at higher levels. The only way to helps learners to remember this information is by repetition and engaging the Taxon memory system.
2   The speed and ease of engaging all learners makes flash-card learning effective and enjoyable.
3   The Rule of Three states that, in order to learn something, it must be repeated at least three times.

## Questions to Consider

1   How will I engage my learners using repetitive comprehension and knowledge-based questions?

_____

_____

_____

2   What other methods of rapid repetition will I use besides flashcards for learners to acquire knowledge and comprehension information?

_____

_____

_____

_____

_____

_____

_____

_____

_____

## Notes

1   The Common Core State Standards initiative uses "anchor skills" in English and "practice skills" in math to indicate fundamental skills that need to be mastered (trained) to be effective in the other content and skills. www.corestandards.org/
2   I've said many times over the years that if all teachers taught like excellent foreign language teachers, we would have students able to converse fluently in math, science, history, and, yes, even English.
3   Popcorn-style questioning is rapid-fire cold-calling, where students do not raise hands. Doug Lemov, in his book, *Teach Like a Champion 2.0* (2015), demonstrates how to keep all students engaged by creating this sense of urgency in asking quick questions.

## Reference

Lemov, D. (2015). *Teach like a champion 2.0*. San Francisco, CA: Wiley.

# Section II

## Planning Learning Conclusion

I have always said that a good lesson always begins with a good lesson plan. The same could be said about questions. Effective questions require that they be thought-out and designed while you are planning your lesson (WILD HOG them). In this section we looked at various aspects of preparing questions for learners at all levels. With advanced planning to include the different needs of your learners, your questioning skills can be effective, causing your participants to learn at increasingly higher levels.

Repeated themes in this section are the ideas of question progressions, tiers, scaffolding, engagement of all learners, repetition, and digging deeper. Invest a few minutes in thoughtfully creating your own learning plan to improve your skills in the following areas. Don't forget to look at the end notes for each chapter for additional sources of learning that you may want to include in your plan.

Section II Planning Learning Professional Growth Plan

| Professional Growth Activity | Resources Needed | Due Date |
|---|---|---|
| 1. WILD HOG Questions | | |
| | | |
| | | |
| 2. A Question for Every Brain | | |
| | | |
| | | |

| Professional Growth Activity | Resources Needed | Due Date |
|---|---|---|
| 3. What Are Effective Ways to Write Questions? | | |
| | | |
| | | |
| 4. How to Scaffold Questions | | |
| | | |
| | | |
| 5. Knowledge and Comprehension Questions | | |
| | | |
| | | |

## Reference

Lemov, D. (2015). *Teach Like a Champion 2.0*. San Francisco, CA: Wiley.

# Section III
## Learning

The act of instruction has been the focus of professional development and training for so many years that many have lost sight that the real point of instruction is actually learning. If what we do as instructors does not actually foment learning, then we are wasting our time and the learners'. In order to be successful at inspiring learning, educators of all types must identify what they believe about how individuals learn best and then align their instruction to match those beliefs. Unfortunately, a wide gap exists between what educators; professors, instructors, facilitators, trainers, and "teachers" say they believe about learning and how they actually promote learning in their professions. This is especially true when it comes to asking questions.

In this section, make sure that you take the time to realign your beliefs with your instructional actions so that your questioning can be as effective at inspiring learning as possible.

# 11

## The Role of Repetition in Questions

### How Can Questions Help Participants Remember Better?

One of my favorite childhood stories was narrated by the famous Danny Kaye. It was a vinyl record (that dates me) of him as a story teller. We wore that record out. The name of the story was "The Tale of the Name of The Tree," and it was a Bantu tale[1] about a community of animals that had a problem. As in most animal tales, they could all talk. None of them could remember the name of the magical tree that provided food to the village. They decided to send the fastest animal up to talk to the wise man on the mountain, but it forgot the name on the way down. The same happened to the smartest, cleverest, and strongest until they decided to send the turtle. At every obstacle the other animals had encountered, the turtle pronounced the name of the tree and, thus, by repeating the name, he was able to save the village. Over the course of the story, the name of the tree is repeated nine times. I was a child when I heard this story, and I can still remember the name of the tree. When something is placed in context that is enjoyable and is repeated multiple times, it will stick.

We have a memory system that is ideal for helping us learn facts, figures, dates, names, vocabulary, symbols, lists, procedures, and just about anything. It is used extensively, almost to exclusion in K–12 public education. Often it is referred to as the "rote" memory system. Another name for it is the Taxon memory system. It takes advantage of our brain's capacity to develop dendrites—or electrochemical pathways—(memories) as a response to continued, repetitive attempts to recall information. It is a physiological response in that the brain actually becomes denser with more dendrites (see also

Section 3.2). To engage the Taxon memory system, simply repeat the information until it sticks, like the name of the tree. Unfortunately, some educators have abused this, and instead of making the repetition enjoyable, interesting, and lively, they have made it drudgery through worksheets, drill and kill programs, and boring recitation. Thus, while learners possess this powerful learning tool, "rote" learning has become anathema to education, though, interestingly enough, education continues to rely heavily on Taxon memory learning—i.e. through the reliance on Level 1 fact-based questioning—and rarely enters the Locale learning realm.

## 11.1  How to Make Taxon Learning Enjoyable Through Questions

As demonstrated with the Bantu tale, repetition can be interesting and enjoyable. Using questions as the main learning enhancing tool, instructors can use the power of Taxon learning in engaging and fun ways. Simple and quick recall questions that ask the learners to demonstrate knowledge and understanding in a game, such as "Simon Says," can be repeated day after day, and the learners enjoy it and even love the challenge of doing better and not being tricked by the instructor or a learner selected to lead the group in the game. Though not strictly questions, "Simon Says" commands form the same function as asking, "Where is . . . ?" or "What is . . . ?"

"Simon says, touch the cranium"
"Simon says, touch the fibula."
"Simon says, touch the occipital nerve."
"Simon says, touch the clavicle."
"Simon says, touch a part of your body that contains cartilage."
"Simon says, touch the frontal lobe."
"Simon says, touch the left Achilles tendon."
"Touch your epiglottis."
"Touch the gluteus maximus."
"Simon says, touch with your left index the location of Wernicke's area.[2]"
"Simon says, touch with your right inferior digit the location of the reticular formation."
"Simon says, don't raise your left patella."
"Simon says, make a right triangle with your arm."
"Simon says, use a friend to make an equilateral triangle."
"Become parallel to the floor."

"Simon says, take a perpendicular stance."

"Simon says, point to the word on the wall that means overlordship with individual self-government."[3]

"Simon says, point to the word on the wall that means the supreme authority to govern yourself."[4]

"Simon says, point to philosopher who said, "It does not matter what you bear, but how you bear it."[5]

"Simon says, stand beneath the drawing of an 'Endoplasmic Reticulum.' "

"Simon says, point to the names of the two antagonists at the battle of Gettysburg."

As you become expert with this simple game, other words besides point, touch, or make can be added such as tell, ask, answer, draw with your toe, write in the air, sit, stand, demonstrate, trace, perform, recite, or dance; as well as positional words, above, beyond, beneath, beside, on, under, next to, behind, adjacent, oblique, tangent, diagonal, or congruent; along with adverbs such as languidly, with alacrity, lugubriously, ponderously, or expeditiously. There are many other engaging games that can help learners answer questions to push short-term memory into long-term memory.[6] The key, though, is that they are part of the learning, not just a review game for special occasions when there is nothing else to do. The game does not need to take up the whole learning time, either.

## 11.2 Questioning Progressions

Keep the power of repetition in mind when you prepare your questions. You don't have to pose the same question nine times, but you can rephrase the question in multiple ways over time. If you recall, in the previous chapter, I mentioned the Rule of Three. The Rule of Three states: *You cannot expect a learner to remember anything just asking about it one time. Only having posed questions on the topic at least three times should you expect them to remember the topic.* This is directly related to Taxon memory and memorization (see Section 3.2). The best way to employ the Rule of Three is to make a WILD HOG tier of questions about the concept you want the learners to remember (learn), easy to hard (see Section 8.2). For example:

Level 1: "When and where did Alexander the Great live?"
Level 1: "What countries did Alexander the Great conquer?"

Level 2: "What was unique about Alexander the Great's achievements?"

Level 2: "What characteristic did Alexander the Great display when he was asked to untie the Gorgon Knot?"[7]

Level 3: "What other historical person could you compare to Alexander the Great?

Level 3: "Alexander the Great died when he was 32. What might he have accomplished if he had died at old age?"

As mentioned in Chapter 17, a wonderful tool for repetition is to ask questions as entrance or exit tickets. The sponge, or "do this while I get things ready" part of instruction is a perfect time to inject repeated questions that need to be remembered (learned). Additionally, if participants get a question wrong, it becomes a formative opportunity to give them another chance to get it right. Formative assessments[8] don't have to be quizzes and tests, as long as the learner has multiple opportunities to improve (see Chapter 17). The word "formative" implies that the learners are the ones growing. The only way for the learners to grow in formative assessments is if they understand their mistakes and have opportunities to take the assessment again. A rough-draft is a formative assessment.

## Summary
1   Repetition is the purview of Taxon memory and knowledge and comprehension. Through repetition, short-term memory is transformed into long-term memory.
2   Repetition does not have to be boring or drudgery, as the term "rote" learning has come to imply. Repetition can be enjoyable and even challenging with a simple game, such as "Simon Says."
3   Repetitive questions do not have to be repetitive. Using the same topic, questions can be tiered according to difficulty and complexity.

## Questions to Consider
1   How will I employ the Rule of Three in my current instruction?

_____

_____

_____

2   What games will I use or devise to provide the necessary repetition in my current instruction?

_____

_____

_____

_____

3   How will I create a question progression tier using the same concepts?

_____

_____

_____

_____

Level 1:

_____

_____

_____

_____

Level 2:

_____

_____

_____

_____

Level 3:

_____

_____

_____

_____

## Notes

1 "The Tale of the Name of the Tree" was written by Pattie Price in her book, *Bantu Tales Retold by Pattie Price* (1938) and combined in a story book called *Danny Kaye's Stories from Far Away Places* (Random House, 1960). Here is a video of the audio of Danny Kaye telling the story: https://youtu.be/eskB_ds9TAk

2 Wernicke's area, the speech center of the brain located in the temporal lobe (left side of the brain), see www.britannica.com/science/Wernicke-area

3 Suzerainty, see www.worldatlas.com/what-is-suzerainty.html

4 Sovereignty, see www.britannica.com/topic/sovereignty

5 Seneca see www.ancient-literature.com/rome_seneca.html

6 Turn whole-class games, where one student at a time participates, into partner games, where both have to participate: *Jeopardy*, *Who Wants to Be a Millionaire?*, $1000 pyramid, *Wheel of Fortune*, Boggle, charades, password, battle ship, Trivial Pursuit, etc. Relay races where each person completes part of a process on the board or on a piece of paper that is passed backwards in the row of seats and the last learner in the row raises the paper when done or Slap it or Snap matching game with vocabulary and definition cards could be used with synonyms or antonyms. Partners simultaneously put down cards; if there is a match, the first to slap their hand on the pile gets all the cards. Fruit bowl: each learner has an assigned term; multiple learners with the same term is OK. Learners sit in a circle with chairs. One learner reads the definition and corresponding learners have to exchange seats; the last one standing has to read the next clue and try to get a seat. Quizlet, Kahoots, or other phone-based games also work, see https://solutionsuggest.com/kahoot-alternatives/.

7 More about the Gorgon knot: www.history.com/news/what-was-the-gordian-knot

8 I looked at five different "expert" books on formative assessments, and some mentioned that the idea behind formative assessments was to help the learner. Most looked at it as a process for teachers to get and give feedback. In my definition of formative assessment, it is all about the learner and learning. "How do you learn to ride a bike?" is real formative assessment.

## Reference

Price, P. (1938), *Bantu Tales Retold by Pattie Price*. New York, NY: E. P. Dutton,

Kaye, D. (1960). *Danny Kaye's stories from far away places*. New York, NY: Random House.

# 12

# Avoiding Zombie Questions

## How Do You Avoid Asking Ineffective Questions?

In this century, education has gone from coercing learners to learn a certain way, as in the "stimulus and response" behaviorism of the 60s, to the time-intensive learner-centered focus of the developmental era of the 80s.[1] In our current political era of standardized testing, we fully recognize that both direct instruction and inquiry are useful for specific types of learning activities, but, unfortunately, we have yet to establish an effective balance. It seems that we are right back in the 60s with behaviorism and "Mastery Learning" again. Interestingly enough, that was when the zombie movie *Night of the Living Dead* became popular.[2] Perhaps that was also the birth of the Zombie Questions used all too often in direct instruction. Of course, the antidote to Zombie Questions is WILD HOG Questions that have the capacity to both help direct instruction and to also propel learner-directed learning (see how to write WILD HOG Questions in Chapter 6).

## 12.1 What Are Zombie Questions?

I would define them as questions the instructor asks that even a zombie could answer, but, because learners are not zombies, nobody answers them. The Zombie Questions are one step up from rhetorical questions that don't expect answers, indeed, that do not want answers. Zombie Questions are questions that are too easy, obvious, stupid, redundant, irrelevant, rhetorical, or simply unanswerable, and only brain-dead zombies would try to answer them. See Table 12.1 for a comparison of Zombie Questions and WILD HOG Questions. When instructors are asking the whole class questions with no forethought about why, to whom the questions are directed, or what is wanted

**Table 12.1** List of Zombie Questions and Corrections

Zombie Questions That Should Never Be Asked

| Often-Used Zombie Questions | The meaning and a *better question* |
| --- | --- |
| Do you understand? | This means "I'm going on if you don't say anything." *Turn to your elbow partner and tell them what you understand about . . .* |
| Any questions? | This means "I'm done." *I'll give you 30 seconds to write your question on a post-it and put it in the "parking lot" on the wall.* |
| Who knows the answer? | This means "I expect not many know the answer." *Stand up if you think you know the answer.* |
| Who can tell me? | Same. *Tell your partner the answer to this question.* |
| Are you ready? | Rhetorical. *In 30 seconds we will go on, so finish up your thoughts.* |
| Will you be quiet? | Rhetorical. *Please be quiet in 10, 9, 8, 7. . . . Thank you.* |
| Can you hear me? | If I can't I won't respond. *If you can hear my voice, raise your left hand.* |
| Can I help you? | Rhetorical. *What can I do to help you?* |
| What is your problem? | Rhetorical. *Can you tell me what your concern is?* |
| Can I have your attention? | Rhetorical. *Same as previous questions.* |

from the questions, that is when we can see Zombie Questions rising from their unmarked tombs.

## 12.2 Learners Are Not Blank Slates

First of all, as instructors, we need to come to grips with the fact that we really do not know everything, and we need to accept the corollary assumption that the learners are not blank slates (sorry, John Locke, no tabula rasa here) and that they actually have some knowledge and skills. So, if we don't know everything and there is no reason to assume that learners know nothing, then it stands to reason that if we ask questions, the learners might give answers that we do not yet know! A scary thought! Well, not really; it is an exciting thought, because when learners are asking questions, then that means that they are ready to learn (by the way, it is OK for instructors to learn right alongside of the learners). Anyway, it is critical, therefore, that learners be able to answer and ask questions, because that helps the learners and the instructors learn (see Chapter 14).

All of this presupposes that instructors have created effective questions that are worth being answered. The point I want to make again is that the instructor must prepare the WILD HOG Questions beforehand, otherwise, research shows that instructors will typically ask low-level, fact-based questions and never get to the level of difficulty that involves analysis and beyond, or the level of complexity that deals with concepts. This type of question can easily turn into Zombie Questions that no one wants to answer.

## 12.3 Why Learners Don't Answer Zombie Questions

We have all been in learning situations in which we have been asked questions that no one wants to answer for a number of reasons. The question may have seemed rhetorical and did not seem that it needed an answer, like "Any questions?" It may have been a question that was too simplistic, and the only appropriate answer would be "Duh!" It might be a question that everyone knows, but no one wants to show off. They might be a series of questions so pedantic that they are a waste of time to answer. Or on the other end of the scale, it could be a question so complex and intricate that the only appropriate answer is "Huh?" A Zombie Question is one that fails to elicit an appropriate response from anyone. Most often, Zombie Questions occur in whole-group questions when the instructor barely knows more than the learners, is unprepared for the instruction, or is incompetent (see examples in Table 12.1).

I witnessed a series of Zombie Questions when I was the assistant superintendent visiting a history class. I walked in with the principal and saw an instructor sitting behind his desk working on his computer while the students were chatting and were supposed to be answering questions from the end of the chapter. As we walked in, the shocked teacher immediately stood up and started asking the students wonderful thought-provoking questions. The students were caught off guard and did their best to try to answer the teacher's questions, but they failed. The teacher tried to help them by giving them leading questions to get them to answer correctly. In exasperation, the teacher just told them the answers and went on asking Zombie Questions with the same result. In this case the students were not accustomed to having to answer such high-level questions and therefore did not have the skill or knowledge to do so.

**Summary**
1   Zombie Questions are ones that fail to elicit appropriate responses for several reasons, but most result from poor or inadequate planning on the part of the instructor.
2   Even good questions can be Zombie Questions if the learners are not prepared to answer them.

**Questions to Consider**

1   How will I avoid using Zombie Questions in my current assignment?

_____

_____

_____

_____

_____

_____

_____

_____

_____

_____

_____

_____

## Note

1   (Wallace & Hurst, 2009).
2   George Romero created *Night of the Living Dead* in 1968, and since then interest in zombies has grown. Due to TV shows like *The Walking Dead* and movies like *World War Z*, *28 Days Later*, and *Shaun of the Dead*, zombies have now become, as Annalee Newitz calls them, "the new vampires." She also makes some incredible connections between the number of zombie movies made as correlated to the amount of political unrest, destruction, and turmoil in the world. Though I am skeptical . . . there might be some truth there. See http://io9.com/a-history-of-zombies-in-america-5692719.

## Reference

Wallace, R., & Hurst, B. (2009). Why do teachers ask questions? Analyzing responses from 1967, 1987, and 2007. *Journal of Reading Education*, 35(1), 39–46. Retrieved December 12, 2011, from http://ehis.ebscohost.com/eds

# 13

# Misconceptions About Asking Questions

## How Can Questions Engage All Learners?

The first misconception is that, for some reason, we believe that we can create effective questions while we are instructing. The bitter truth is that not only is this impossible to do well, but the act of trying to do it diminishes our performance in inspiring learning for all participants; the questions are low-quality, nonengaging, and cater to just a few learners. At the same time, it also brings us dangerously close to "hog wild" questions; not having a question plan we may go "hog wild," we get off track, and we lose focus. WILD HOG Questions are deliberately created before instruction and are targeted for maximum effect. It is extremely difficult to come up with higher-order thinking questions while we are monitoring the learners' behavior, trying to engage all learners, and keeping the momentum of learning going. Research shows that a large majority of the questions that instructors ask on the fly (intellectually known as intuitive questions) are pure knowledge-based questions (aka Zombie Questions—see previous chapter).[1] This is the reason why instructors should spend time crafting excellent WILD HOG Questions before instruction (see Chapter 6).

> *WILD HOG Questions are questions that, just like the feral pigs, multiply and create more questions. They are unpredictable, voracious, and challenging.*

Another misconception is the belief that, if instructors are asking questions to individual learners or directing a classroom discussion, the whole group of learners is learning. Nothing could be further from the truth. Research shows that questions asked to the whole group are minimally effective (we'll talk about this a bit more in section 13.3 How do You Use Questions to Engage More Than the Front Row?).

Parallel to the prior misconception is the following: there is the commonly held belief among instructors that if we are not asking questions, we are not teaching. A few years ago, the stereotypical instructor used to stand in front of the room and alternate between pointing to the blackboard and providing important facts for learners to remember and asking questions to make sure the learners had acquired the important facts. Today, the stereotypical instructor does almost the exact same thing but now wanders around that classroom with a PowerPoint controller or virtual mouse to control the screen. In either case, the instructor is doing all of the work. The seated learners are supposed to be intensely alert and thoroughly attentive . . . but because they are only asked to passively participate in the learning (i.e. voluntarily answering questions, optional notes), most of the learners are only partially listening, and of those listening (the academically inclined learners), most are only halfway paying attention.

## The Fallacy of Whole-Group Questions

If we look at the dynamics of any classroom, it doesn't take more than a week for learners to figure out who they think is smart, who is not, and who doesn't care. In most cases, the learners have known their classmates for years. What is more telling, studies show that after fourth grade, learners know how they are perceived and play their roles accordingly.[2] Looking at things from the learners' perspective about the questions posed in the classroom, we can see why non-WILD HOG Questions are not as effective as we would like them to be. If you remember from Chapter 6, in the creation of WILD HOG Questions, we have to consider the audience when we make the question. If we know that learners behave according to their perceptions of themselves, we should not ignore those perceptions but rather design questions to target individual learners. All too often, instructors instead proffer questions to the entire class and, in the spirit of volunteerism, the instructors wait for the learners who want to answer to raise their hands. Here is an example of such a whole-group question ostensibly designed to make a typical group of learners think:

"Class, if you could stretch string from here to the moon, how many balls of string would it take?"

After hearing this question, the learners who know they are not the "smart ones" are not going to take the bait. Neither will the learners who do not care about the moon or balls of string. Both of these groups of learners, unless otherwise motivated, will sit back and watch what happens. This leaves the learners who think they are "smart" or those that really are "smart" as the only ones possibly interested in answering.

Some of the truly intelligent learners have been burned before, so they will not be answering the question. These intelligent learners may have been exposed to other learners mocking them for being so "smart" or have been abused by instructors who unwittingly make examples of them, use them as tutors, or constantly pair them with the most struggling learners. For some of these "smart" learners, being smart is a liability; it means more work, less enjoyment, and it means they never get to be in groups with their friends. Just like in the military or even worse, in the faculty meetings at school, they learn rather quickly to not volunteer.

Back to the example, almost before the question is completely stated, one or two eager learners already have their hands up with an answer, right or wrong. The other groups of learners are perfectly fine with this routine. Most likely, they are thinking to themselves, "Better them than me! Let the smart kids answer the questions so I don't have to." It is difficult for an instructor to resist the learners in the front, waving their hands. When no one else volunteers, however, the instructor usually relents.

We instructors may defend the practice of asking whole-group questions because the motivated learner who always answers the questions will help the whole group to learn the right answer. There could be some truth in this way of thinking . . . *if* the whole class were really listening! In reality, though, this line of thought is naïve and seriously misguided in terms of what is going on in the learners' minds. When the instructor starts pacing the room, hand rubbing their chin, the learners know the drill. The instructor is going to start asking questions. If the learners know from past experience that the questions will be open to the entire class, then most likely two-thirds of the class will not even pay it any attention and continue doodling or daydreaming because they know who will try to answer the questions. It makes no difference how well constructed the questions or how relevant or engaging they might be. If they are whole-group questions, they will fall mainly on deaf ears.

## Misconception of Rigor

A misconception I would like to identify is that we often believe that "rigor at all costs" is acceptable. This means that we think that it is OK to get learners to think by any means possible, including trickery, emotionally charged topics, and purposeful confusion (for instance, the "devil's advocate"). When we do this, we actually do more harm than good to participant learning. Questions that purposefully mislead learners or play with their understanding only train learners to overanalyze and misinterpret the truth because it is too obvious. According to Erickson's Concept-Based

Curriculum (Erickson, Lanning, & French, 2017) that relates to complexity of thinking, with different types of knowledge, question difficulty can be arrived at by moving from Fact to Topic and from Topic to Concept, then to Principle and Generalization, until the knowledge of Theory is obtained.[3] Also increasing question complexity (multistep or multifaceted questions) and correlating them to the learner's current conceptual understanding will increase rigor (see Chapter 6, Learning Depth). Rigorous, (difficult and complex) questions should be aimed at helping learners to synthesize knowledge rather than having the learners guess about nitpicky minutia. Knowledge is important, and understanding knowledge correctly is also important, but it is easy to get lost in the details and thus never get to the overall understanding learners need.

## 13.1 Initiate–Respond–Evaluate: How Do You Avoid the One Question, One Answer Trap?

I start this section by stating that every learner deserves to answer great questions. The problem is that most learners are not given the chance. To illustrate this, I would like to share an interesting experience. I was the assistant superintendent in a small school district, and I had a lot of liberty. I was curious to see the perspective of the students who go to our schools and realized that I could not get this from 5-minute spot checks. To this end, I spent a week and shadowed students in my district. I went to all of their classes just as they would. Among some other very interesting observations, I discovered that during the course of a day in departmentalized classrooms some students would go from class to class and never answer (or ask) a single question all day long. Teachers did not catch on to this because they did not know what went on in the class prior and therefore did not see that these students never participated in that class either. (These students, by the way, are experts at traveling under the radar. They don't make noise, don't cause a fuss or disrupt the class, so they never draw attention to themselves. Thinking back, I probably was one of those students when I was younger . . . hmmm.) Anyway, this problem is not isolated to a particular grade level; I saw it in several, and now that I know what I am looking for I see it in every grade level. Effective use of questions would fix this travesty in a jiffy.

> *Some students would go from class to class and never answer (or ask) a single question all day long*

There are simple ways to keep these silent learners on the radar, and the first step is to recognize that this happens more than we would like to admit. The second step is to commit to engaging every learner with awesome WILD HOG Questions. As an example of this, I want to show you different sides of the same seventh-grade lesson on photosynthesis in order to contrast two teachers and their approach to engaging every learner brain with questions.

### Teacher X and the Photosynthesis Lesson

Students file into his seventh-grade classroom and take their seats. Teacher X stands up in front of the room and welcomes them. Then X directs them to the sponge activity to keep them occupied while he takes roll and checks homework. X introduces the three learning objectives for today on the whiteboard. The objective as written states: "The student is expected to recognize that radiant energy from the sun is transformed into chemical energy through the process of photosynthesis."

Teacher X is eager to get into the subject matter for today's lesson: plant energy cycles (TEKS 7(b)5A). X begins by asking the class questions about the plant energy cycles. His idea is to start with easy questions to get the students thinking: animals get energy from eating food. What do plants eat? How do plants get energy? Then, depending on the answers, he will go on to more difficult questions: What do all plants have in common? Why are plants green? What does the color green have to do with plant's energy? How do plants get nutrients? Then he will show them pictures of plants, plant leaves, plant cells, and chloroplasts. Then he will ask them to show what they know by identifying the plant parts related to photosynthesis and how they work in the creation of ATP.

Teacher X asks his first question. "Animals get energy from eating plants; what do plants eat?"

Some students raise their hands. Most just look at him. Teacher X asks one of the boys frantically waving his hand in the front of the room. "Charles, you look like you know the answer."

"They eat dirt!"

"Well, that is not precisely the right answer. Does anyone else have another idea of what plants eat?"

"Plants eat people!" one boy answers coyly, "I saw it in a movie!"

After getting the class to stop laughing, Teacher X persists. "Yes there are carnivorous plants, but none large enough to eat people."

"But if people are buried, and plants grow on top of them, don't they eat people then?" one student conjectures. Now, X is sorry that he compared animals eating to plants eating!

"Yes, you have a point there. But who can tell me how plants get their energy?"

"No one else? What about you Joe, what do you think?"

"I don't know, sir."

"How about you Sally? Where do plants get their food?"

"Oh, I get it! They get it from fertilizer! That is why we have plant food!"

"Well, yes we do buy fertilizer for plants and sometimes we call that 'plant food.'" X tries another tact, "But . . . do any of you have plants inside your house?"

A few hands are raised tentatively.

"Ok, what happens to the plants when you leave on vacation?"

"They dry up and wilt. That's it isn't it! They get their food from the water!"

"No, the water is not their food. Alright. Let me just tell you. Plants get their food from the sun." Teacher X tells the students resignedly.

Now some of the students look strangely at him. A hand goes up, "What does the sun have to do with feeding plants?"

"Because plants are green, plants can use a process called photosynthesis to convert energy from the sun's light to sugar! Do you want to know how that works?"

"Plants eat light?"

"Oh forget it. Here is the worksheet."

## A Student Perspective on the Photosynthesis Lesson

Joe obediently sits down and waits for the instructor to tell him what to do. Joe sees the objective on the board but doesn't pay it any attention. It doesn't make much sense to him because it is written in teacher-speak. The teacher is obviously excited about something. OK, he is going to ask some questions. Don't make eye contact and he won't call on you.[4]

Good, he called on Charles who always raises his hand. Plants eat food? That's weird. What's he after? I really don't feel like answering questions now.

Rats, Charles took my answer. OK, he got it wrong.

Wrong again. Why doesn't the teacher just tell us what he wants us to know?

Oh, no. I looked at him. He is going to ask me. "I don't know sir." I get so nervous when the teacher asks me questions. Sometimes my mind goes blank when teachers do that. I forget everything, even if I know the answer.

But now I really don't know what the teacher wants. He is so confusing. First he says one thing then he says another. Plants eat food, but they don't eat inside the house?

Finally! He's giving up. Look how much time he wasted. He should have just given us the worksheet right at the start.

### Teacher Y and the Photosynthesis Lesson

Teacher Y: "What do plants eat?"

Some students raise their hands, most just look at Y. Y asks one of the boys frantically waving his hand in the front of the room. "Charles, you look like you know the answer."

"They eat dirt!"

"Well, that is not precisely the right answer. But how could we find out what plants eat if they eat at all?"

"We could perform an experiment," a girl conjectures.

"Great idea! Let's all go outside to do an experiment, but first I have to prepare you for the experiment. You are all going to pretend to be plants. Your faces will be the leaves of your plant. No, we will not paint your faces green, but you have to imagine that they are full of chloroplasts—the organelles within plant cells that make the leaves look green. Next you need to bring your field notebook and a pencil. Ready? OK, let's go to the field."

Teacher Y gives instructions, "Everyone sit on the grass please. OK, close your eyes. Remember, your faces are the leaves of the plants. What do you all feel on your face? Just say it out loud, all at once."

"The wind."

"Coldness."

"Yes, there is a slight wind. What else do you feel?"

The students do not respond for a moment.

"OK, here comes the experiment. Raise your field notebooks above your head to shade your face. Now what do you feel?"

All the students respond in general, "It feels cooler."

"Everyone, tell your neighbor why you think it feels cooler."

The general consensus was, "Because the notebook blocked the sun."

Teacher Y notes that he needs to correct some thinking, "The notebook would burn up if it blocked the sun. Everyone, what was it really that notebook blocks?"

"Ahhhh! Light from the sun."

"Now lower the notebooks. Ask your partners, 'Now, what do you feel?' "

In general the students agree, "I feel heat from the sun."

"Describe to your partner what heat is."

Teacher Y then asks the students to make a judgment, "If you think that heat is a form of energy, raise your notebooks in the air."

All notebooks rise.

"If you think dirt is a form of energy, raise your notebooks in the air."

No notebooks are lifted.

"Now turn to your elbow partner, and in 30 seconds discuss how animals get their energy to survive"

In chorus, the students respond, "They eat living things."

"Wonderful! You remember the food cycle. If eating is the way animals get their energy, how do plants get their energy?

"The sun."

Teacher Y feels he needs to get the students to be precise, "Remember, the sun would burn them up. How do plants get their energy from the sun?"

"They soak up light from the sun."

"Back to my first question. Class, what do plants eat?"

All the students respond, "They eat light from the sun."

"Do plants eat?"

"No, they soak up light from the sun!"

"Again, what do plants eat?"

In unison they reply, "They don't eat. They soak up light from the sun."

"That is correct. Take a minute to write down in your field notebook how we learned that plants get energy from the sun's light. When we go inside again, we will learn how the green chloroplasts in plant leaves turn the sun's light energy into food using ATP."

## Analysis of a Lesson on Photosynthesis

Both teacher X and teacher Y asked good questions. What made the difference? Only one main thing . . . *how* the teachers used the questions. Teacher X had a solid plan, but neglected to put himself in the shoes of the students and try to think how they might respond to his questions. As a result, the lesson lost momentum and the teacher, as even I have done in similar situations, gave into what was easier, rather than what was most important. Teacher Y, on the other hand, began with the same question and took it in a whole different direction. Teacher Y combined the questions with effective small- and whole-group strategies and a change of scenery to help students learn. Teacher X depended on "one student at a time" discussions while Teacher Y helped students ask their own questions to each other. Most importantly, Teacher Y used questions to get students thinking.

## Summary
1   Learners deserve to be asked great questions.
2   Typical whole-group questions are actually conversations between the instructor and one willing learner.

3   Rigor does not mean instructing the learner on how to answer tricky, misleading questions. It means creating questions that cause the learner to think deeply in order to answer. These questions are designed to use higher-order thinking, concept knowledge, and complexity.

4   Some learners successfully evade answering questions all day long.

5   Teacher X shows that engaging one learner at a time is inefficient and makes other learners wait their turn. Additionally, from Teacher X's perspective, he had a solid "teaching" plan, but he was the one trying to get the information in the heads of the learners, while Teacher Y engages them all at the same time and shows that active learning requires questions that are active. Teacher Y makes it fun for the learners. The difference was that the learners were answering their own questions.

6   Before committing to a series of questions, consider how your learners will respond to them first.

## Questions to Consider

1   What alternatives will I use to avoid the whole-class question in my instruction?

_____

_____

_____

2   How do I clarify my questions to avoid misunderstandings and confusion?

_____

_____

_____

_____

3   What can I do to avoid the one question, one answer trap?

_____

_____

_____

_____

4    How can I follow the example of Teacher Y and engage my learners in active learning through my questions in my current instruction?

_____

_____

_____

_____

_____

_____

_____

_____

_____

_____

## 13.2  The Fallacy of Wait Time: How Do You Stop Wasting Time Waiting for Participants to Answer?

### Wait Time

So, how do instructors ask a question the right way? One crutch strategy was developed by Mary Budd Rowe in the 1980s. We call it "wait time." I call it a "crutch" strategy because it is trying to make the best out of a poor classroom instructional activity: whole-group questions. While you may be tired of my fictitious scenarios, I am going to risk one more—in advance please pardon the repetition of some common themes.

Let's say a novice instructor, Joe, notices the problems associated with whole-group questions and decide something has to change. He decides to ask particular students questions. So, he singles out a specific student for his new tactic of asking questions.

"Jeffry. What is the difference between zombies and patched jeans?"[5]

Several hands in the front of the class slowly recede as they realize that the question has been assigned to Jeffrey. All eyes are on Jeffry. Well, some eyes are on Jeffry. The rest of the students just breathed sighs of relief that their names were not called. The question asked is not their problem, and neither is the answer.

(Joe, the novice instructor, naively believes that, while Jeffry is thinking of the answer, the rest of the students are also thinking. Wouldn't that be nice? What Joe, the novice instructor, doesn't realize is that at best one-third of the students are thinking about an answer and the rest are just glad they are not in the spotlight.)

Jeffry struggles to answer immediately, Joe, the novice instructor, quickly targets another student. Now Jeffry is off the hook, and another student is sweating in the limelight. Yet, even still, few students are listening to the question, and even fewer are looking for an answer. Joe continues asking students until no student guesses the correct answer and Joe, the novice instructor, gives up and just tells the students the answer.

Joe the novice teacher says in frustrated tones, "Remember this, it is going to be on the quiz. Zombies are dead men, and the patched jeans are mended (men dead)." (I know, it wasn't worth waiting for, sorry.)

Many of us have been exposed to the questioning strategies researched by Mary Budd Rowe. She proposed that instructors simply ask a question, such as "What do you call it when an insect kills itself?" pause for at least three seconds, and then say a student's name: "Sally."

By stating the question without assigning it to a student immediately, all the students will automatically be thinking about how they would answer the question because they don't know who is going to be asked the question, and it might be them. Then, only after another child's name is said, will they sigh in relief because they were not chosen. But they did think for a few seconds, and that makes a little difference.

The fallacy is assuming that all students will be thinking. There is no way to know, but my own experience tells me that we are lucky if a few were thinking. I suppose that is better than none.

## Asking Every Participant Questions

Luckily, there are multitudes of ways of asking questions, other than whole-group questions, that will entice and inspire learners to voluntarily participate in answering and asking questions, as we will see later.

Don't get me wrong. It is OK to ask questions to the "whole group" if the whole group answers. We need to recognize, however, that the problem with "whole-group" questions is the *way* the question is asked: only one learner at a time (which really isn't whole group, is it?). If a "discussion" results in poor learner participation and low knowledge retention, it is not necessarily the questions that are at fault. The point is that in order to increase participant learning we must use WILD HOG Questions to involve the "whole class" rather than just one or two learners at a time.

As stated earlier, the problem with whole-class questions might not be the question at all; it is how the question is asked. In a typical classroom where the instructor asks a question to a learner, while the one learner is engaged to a certain extent in answering the question, what are the other learners doing?

Who knows?

We can identify the ones who are obviously not listening and don't care that we see their disdain. We can surmise that the ones with their heads on their desks probably are not listening either. That leaves us with the learners who are not looking at the instructor but are intent on writing, drawing, or scribbling and the small group of learners who are actually looking at the instructor and doing nothing else. There is no way to know what is going on in their minds. Some instructors might incorrectly assume that all the learners looking at the instructor are listening, while all of the learners not looking at the instructor are not listening. Listening is a passive activity and in and of itself; it is a poor learning tool.

In order to increase learner participation, it may work for some instructors (of younger learners especially) to tell the learners beforehand that, when questions are asked, each learner is expected to be able to respond to the question. Older learners may not respond to this unless there is a reason to do so, i.e. participation points (mainly online learners), grades, etc. In some classrooms, I have seen that it is expected that every learner should raise their hand when a question is asked.[6] If all learners in the class raised their hands, it is the same as if no learner raised his or her hand. As a result, the instructor will probably use the traditional reasons for selecting learners to answer questions: choose a learner whom the instructor believes knows the answer or choose a learner whom the instructor believes should be paying more attention.

## Choral Response

By far the easiest solution to engage *all* learners in learning is to actually ask a list of WILD HOG Questions to the whole class and have the whole class answer the questions out loud—all at the same time. This is known as choral response. This is different from an instructor saying a phrase and asking the class to repeat the phrase, exactly as stated by the instructor. When learners respond chorally, all of the answers may be correct, but they do not have to be said the same way, using the same words. As a matter of fact, it is preferable that the answers are different. Answering with the whole class at the same time, a learner has little reason to fear humiliation, shame, or embarrassment. The affective filter—or emotional risk factor, according to Krashen (1986)—is as low as it can get.[7] While the learners are all answering the questions, the instructor should roam the classroom as questions are answered and listen for the answers of the learners, perhaps asking sections of the class to repeat their answers for learners who may not be totally correct. Based on the over-heard responses of the learners, the instructor can rephrase the questions or break the questions down to help the "whole class" refine their answers. As necessary, the instructor can take a moment and do a mini teach on a particular element, not forgetting to ask the questions again to hear the modified responses and reinforce the learning.

Aside from being noisy, how will having all of the learners say the answer to the question help the learners or the instructor? Let's start with the learners. We can suppose that some of the learners do not know the answer at first. However, they will learn the answer when they hear the rest of the learners say the answer. Struggling learners will automatically look to the learners that they think always have the right answer. The instructor should be alert, however, and watch and listen to make sure the answer is correct. The next time the question is asked, the learner will be able to answer with more confidence (see Chapter 11 on the importance of repetition). The instructor has to remember to make the next time happen, though. Recycling different forms of the questions several times strengthens long-term memory using the Taxon memory system. Making the whole-class questioning fun and ratcheting up the questions' difficulty and complexity uses the Locale memory system, which also enhances long-term memory (see Section 3.2).

The learners who either do not chorally chime in or those that do so hesitantly at first will warm up to the choral response when they see everyone else having fun. As the instructor is roaming about the room, even among all the noise of learners saying the answer, the instructor can clearly hear the learners nearby and their responses. To keep it interesting the instructor can direct the learners to say the answer to their left, to the right, to the floor, the ceiling, whispered, shouted, backwards, in pig Latin, like a robot, like a professional wrestler, on one foot, jumping up and down . . . the combinations are endless.

The premise behind all learners answering is more than simply keeping the learners busy. It is based on the fact that learning is an active endeavor,[8] and the most effective learning uses all of the senses, emotions, and physical extensions of the brain.[9] Early in my career as a Spanish teacher, I learned that the mouth is connected to the brain, and that if I could get the mouth moving, the brain was moving also. I also discovered that if the learners could not pronounce the word out loud, there was no way in the world the learners would ever be able to remember the word. As a fortuitous outcome of the choral response out loud adventure, your learners will begin to be able to speak and understand and converse in the language of mathematics, science, history, or whatever subject you are studying. You will notice this fundamental fact of learning throughout this book: that the body is connected to the brain, and that, if the body is engaged, so is the brain.

## Paired Response

Taking the concept of engaging every learner in answering questions even further, learners can ask and answer questions with their partners, all at the same time. This is more than "Think pair share." One learner listens and corrects, while the other explains, and then they switch. Since repetition is important in learning, a variation of the partner share helps learners to explain several times and listen several times (remember the Rule of Three?). Have the learners line up in two lines, each learner facing the opposite line. The learners explain and listen, and then one line takes a step to the right. The end learner, now without a partner, goes to the other end of the line and the process is repeated. Another interesting way to look at this activity is that, if each learner has a different piece of the puzzle, then shifting through all the learners gives all the learners all of the different pieces of the puzzle. The power behind this approach is that learners are not passively sitting and listening to the instructor.[10] They are actively creating dendrites (connections) and expanding the connections to other dendrites (see Sections 2.4 and 3.2). You read correctly, I affirm that the act of learning is a physiological activity, not just a cognitive one. The brain actually gets bigger the more learning that takes place.[11]

## Keeping Track of Who Answers Questions

Traditionally, creative instructors accompany the "wait time" technique with a system to make sure that every child gets to answer questions in a random fashion. I have seen instructors carry their roll book as they ask questions and simply do a tally mark on the day for each learner that is asked a question. This method has advantages because an instructor has a record of which learner answered questions. Notation can easily be devised to indicate if the learner made the attempt to answer and was successful or not. I have also seen instructors use a cup full of tongue depressors with learners' names on them as a method to randomly choose a learner to answer a question. This is a wonderful way to keep track of who has answered and who has not answered a question simply by removing the depressors as each question is answered. I must provide a caution here. There is a danger that if the learner's names are not kept in the cup, then once the learners answer a question, they will think they have answered their one question and are done for the day. Instructors may avoid this by simply putting the depressors back in the same cup, upside down (learners don't need to know that).

So, in order to get the most effect out of the questions we ask, if we are not planning to use a methodology such as choral repetition to have *all* the learners answer questions at the same time, or elbow partners so half of the learners are answering, or small groups where a quarter of the learners are answering, then at the very least we should be asking a question, pausing for

three seconds, then calling a learner's name—whom we keep track of as having been asked a question—and then pausing again to let the learner answer.
Any questions?

## Summary

1  Choral response is the opportunity to engage all learners in the lowest affective (emotional risk) learning activity.
2  The body is connected to the brain, and, if the body is active, so is the brain. Choral response is a method to engage the whole body of every learner.
3  Paired response activities help learners to engage in learning on a personal level. Done appropriately, learners will be able to become instructors and learners.
4  Some learners go through the whole day and never get asked or answer a single question. Instructors need to be sympathetic to learners who most likely have been sitting and listening all day long.
5  Mary Budd Rowe established that simply giving a pause after a question and then calling on a learner attempts to help all learners to be more engaged in listening to the question and preparing an answer. Wait time also refers to the pause that follows the selection of the learner.
6  Instructors need to devise a way to make sure that every learner has an opportunity to respond to a question: recording who is asked questions on the role sheet, using tongue depressors with learner names, etc.

## Questions to Consider

1  What would I see if I took the place of one of the learners during the week?

_____

_____

_____

_____

2  How do I keep track of which learners answered questions, which refused, and which were successful?

_____

_____

_____

_____

3    What questions will I use to create a choral response progression or paired response progression in my current instruction?

_____

_____

_____

_____

_____

_____

_____

_____

_____

_____

_____

_____

4    How can I hear every learner while they respond chorally? What should I look for?

How do I build on learner success when they answer incorrectly?

_____

_____

_____

_____

_____

_____

_____

_____

_____

_____

## 13.3 Targeted Questions: How Do You Use Questions to Engage More Than the Front Row?

### The Fallacy of Classroom Discussions

As I have explained earlier, the learners know which learners in the class-room will be listening to the instructor and are content to let them deal with the questions the instructor asks in an attempt to get a "discussion" going. Instructors who recognize this disturbing attitude in their classroom questioning may institute measures to try to motivate all learners to participate by attempting to raise the level of urgency. I have learned by experience that making grandiose statements, like the ones to follow, do not impress most learners and do little to change their behavior.

"You will need this information when you get to college."

"This will be on the quiz."

"You will be responsible for knowing this."

"This is part of your participation grade."

More subtle instructors may resort to bribery, embarrassment, or disci-plinary measures to encourage learner participation in whole group questions.

"Ten points to the first person to raise their hand with the right answer."

"Are you guys asleep? Come on, this is an easy question!'

"We will sit here all day until someone other than . . . answers the question."

Frankly, there is nothing that an instructor can do to force learners to volunteer to answer questions posed to the whole class. Let's look at an example.

"Class. . . . Let's talk about the Monroe Doctrine. What do you know?"

One learner replies, "The Monroe Doctrine basically told other nations to stay away from colonizing America."

"What else did it say?"

Different learner replies, "It said the US would get involved if any Euro-pean power should attempt to reconquer or expand liberated or existing colonies."

"Does the US still follow the Monroe Doctrine today?"

Several heads nod, mostly in the front row, "Yes."

"What examples can you give me to show this?"

This appears to be an excellent discussion, but think about how many learners are actually engaged in the previous exchange. At least one learner is involved for each question, and it could be as many as three. Depending on the class, other learners may also be passively engaged in listening, but that is a long shot.

## The Reality of Classroom Discussions

The reality is that some learners maybe are learning, but most aren't. Let me explain why such classroom discussions don't work so well. This type of instructor–learner interaction really is not a classroom "discussion." According to Dr. William Wilen, a professor of social studies at Kent State University, in his article titled "Refuting Misconceptions About Classroom Discussion," this learning activity is actually a "recitation" because one learner at a time is talking with the instructor, who is reviewing material the learners already know, while most of the learners are observers and may or may not be listening. Most crucially, the learners are not in charge of the "discussion." In a recitation, it is the instructor's show all the way. The instructor is typically fishing for the "right answer" and is trying to draw it out of the learners by asking leading questions. Even if the instructor steps out of the recitation mode and lets the learners talk, such impromptu "discussions" only allow learners to provide their opinions with no evidence, little thinking, and less learning.[12]

In true discussion, there is no "leader." There is give-and-take from everyone, and that involves preparation, conjecture, deduction, argument, proofs, and logical conclusions. Most importantly, in a true discussion, the outcome of the discussion is not known beforehand but is discovered through the discussion process. Learners unfamiliar with true discussion or, better stated, learners who only know "recitation" will need some structures to help them participate and be effective in the discussion. Dr. Wilen obligingly shared some strategies that provide the structures to help all learners to be successful in learning from participation in discussions (see Table 13.1).

Along with these other discussion techniques, Socratic Seminars or modified seminars are excellent whole-class/half-class discussion techniques because they are planned in advance and learners have time to prepare evidence and to consolidate their opinions. During the discussion, the role of the instructor is not to lead but to clarify and encourage. Four-corner debates engage more learners at the same time and can enrich the discussion from four different perspectives. Formal debate forces learners to not only prepare their own argument but to consider the opponent's. (I describe these more fully in my book, *Teaching Students to Dig Deeper*.) The success of each of these techniques is dependent on the creation of great WILD HOG Questions.

After understanding this definition of a true discussion, trying to "lead" a class discussion is a waste of effort and time, primarily because "leading" destroys the exploratory purpose of the "discussion" but also because the number of learners that are able to participate in a whole-class recitation is limited to just a few. I think you know where I am going with this: instead of

**Table 13.1** Structures for Engaging All Participants in True Discussions

---

### 1. Response cards.

Pass out index cards and ask for anonymous answers to your discussion questions. Then group the responses to structure specific small-group discussions for each topic, or identify an issue for the class to explore through another set of response cards for discussion.

### 2. Polling.

Use a verbal survey by asking for a show of hands on positions related to an issue. Then follow up the diagnosis of group sentiment with a discussion based on support for positions.

### 3. Whips.

The whip leader goes around the 'group and obtains each participant's' point of view or a random sample of views. Use whips when you want to obtain something quickly from each participant. The information might be used to form small groups representing different perspectives on an issue or solutions to a problem.

### 4. Informal panel.

Invite a small number of participants to present their views in front of the entire class as a panel, and the rest of the learners ask them questions.

### 5. Discussion chip.

Distribute the same number of chips or pennies (three to five) to each member in a small group of students. Tell them that they are to use one chip for every answer, comment, or question as part of a discussion. Participants need to use up all their chips before the discussion is completed or redistribute another equal number of chips for the discussion to continue.

### 6. Talking ball.

Toss a small foam ball to a participant with the understanding that he or she must provide an answer to the discussion question, make a comment, or ask a question. That participant then tosses the ball to another participant, and so on (Passe and Evans 1996; Wilen 1994).

---

"leading" a recitation or even a true discussion, why not teach your learners how to discuss by breaking your class up into groups of four or five learners, so they can then discuss the issues?

Are engaging discussions possible with an elbow partner? Of course they are. Having every learner involved would be much more productive than having 30 or more learners listening to just a few learners talk with the instructor. If instructors could actively involve nearly all of their learners using WILD HOG Questions, would it not increase participant learning? Rhetorical question—of course it would.

Michael Schmoker stated,

Everyday of their school lives, students should be reading texts critically, then weighing evidence for or against people, ideas and policies, and forming opinions. These activities foster a set of essential,
intellectual 'habits of mind' as Meier and author Ted Sizer call them.[13]

Marzano proclaimed, "Arguably, keeping students engaged is one of the
most important considerations for the classroom instructor."[14] Learners need
to be engaged in thinking, and asking WILD HOG Questions is a powerful
way to do that.

The following table is a list of questioning practices that instructors should
avoid (see Table 13.2).

Table 13.2 Whole-Group Question Mistakes to Avoid

**Whole-Group Question Mistakes to Avoid**

| Common Mistakes Made in Asking Whole-Group Questions | Likely Participant Reactions and Solutions |
| --- | --- |
| Rhetorical questions, "Any questions?" | Participants will learn not to answer, so ask specific questions to check understanding. |
| Depending on volunteers to answer questions | Participants will allow others to answer, so ask specific participants or groups of participants to answer the question. |
| Choosing only participants not listening | Participants will pretend to listen, so warn participants that you may call on them to give them time to prepare their answers. |
| Answering one's own questions | Participants simply play dumb and wait for the answer, so instead, ask more questions and never give the answer. |
| Not allowing time for participants to answer | Participants feel frustration, so wait at least five seconds before trying to help the participant find the answer. |
| Not acknowledging participant effort | Participants give up when they realize it doesn't matter, so compliment the participant sincerely, not just "good job." |
| Asking obvious questions (Zombie Questions) | Participants feel insulted, so skip those questions and try harder ones. |

| Common Mistakes Made in Asking Whole-Group Questions | Likely Participant Reactions and Solutions |
| --- | --- |
| Asking only knowledge-level questions | Participants will give only knowledge-level answers, so prepare your higher-level questions in advance. |
| Not following up with more questions | Participants may have incomplete knowledge, so do not let half an answer stand; ask probing questions. |
| Not making sure all participants get a shot at answering questions | Participants fall through the cracks easily, especially shy ones, so make a system so you know every learner answered questions. |

## Four Corners WILD HOG Debates

Conveniently, each room has four corners, and for multiple-choice questions, each corner can represent an answer. As illustrated earlier in TPR, getting learners to move from corner to corner to signify their answer is a great way to get learners' minds and bodies engaged. One rule that must be observed is that, if a learner chooses a corner, they must be able to defend the reason they chose that corner. Interesting discussions can ensue if the instructor knows how to ask questions Socratically. This means that you basically never give the learners the answer. You just keep asking deeper questions to help them figure it out for themselves (in a Socratic Seminar, learners would also be asking a lot of the Socratic questions). Below is a sample list of WILD HOG Questions you will want to jot down before participating in the four corners debate:

**WILD HOG Questions for clarification**
- What do you mean by that?
- How do you define . . . ?
- Could you state your statement in a different way?

**WILD HOG Questions to probe understanding**
- How does that relate to . . . ?
- What other concepts are involved?
- What do you understand by . . . ?

**WILD HOG Questions to incite more learning**
- Where could you find more information about this?
- What other sources did you discover?
- What questions do you have about this?

**WILD HOG Questions to show thinking processes**
- ◆ What did you do to discover this?
- ◆ Why did you follow this train of thought?
- ◆ What steps did you take to get your answer?

**WILD HOG Questions to ask for proof**
- ◆ What evidence supports your thinking?
- ◆ How did you arrive at that conclusion?
- ◆ What is the basis for your statement?

In Figure 13.1, the instructor assigns an answer to the question to each of the four corners of the classroom. The question is purposefully contradictory and requires the learners to "evaluate" (the second most difficult of Benjamin Blooms' cognitive tasks).

> Class, please answer the following question by standing in the corner of the room that best fits what you think. You must choose a corner. Do not simply make your decision based on the number of learners who have already chosen a corner, or by where your friends are because this is not a right or wrong type of question. . . . Now that you have chosen a corner, as a group, you will have 15 minutes to design an experiment that will support what your corner believes.

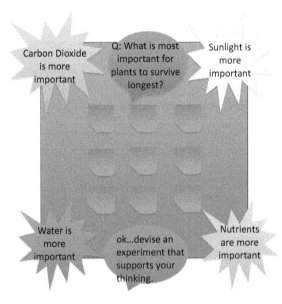

**Figure 13.1** Illustration of a Four Corners Debate

## High- and Low-Tech Response to WILD HOG Questions

Another way to get learners to answer all at once is to either use a high-tech method or a low-tech method. The high-tech method involves the use of "clickers" associated with "Smart" boards, wirelessly connected calculators such as the TI Navigator tools, or having the learners use their phones and respond to questions using Quizlet or Kahoot. Given a question, learners can all answer the question on their device, and the system can tabulate all of the answers that are correct and incorrect immediately. Sophisticated systems can keep track of learner responses over time and inform the instructor of progress for each individual learner and the class in general.

> *If we want all of the learners to know the answer to the questions, isn't it ridiculous to have only one learner at a time answer the questions?*

The low-tech method does not involve batteries and the other headaches of networking technology or dealing with learners distracted by their smart phones. The simplest method is to ask the learners to use give the thumbs up or the thumbs down to show their agreement. Learners can also use their fingers to show the answers as they raise their hands in the air. Another example is to have the learners fold a piece of paper in quarters and write the letters A, B, C, D in each quarter. When a multiple-choice question is given, the learners simply show the instructor the letter of the correct answer. One step above this, crayons can be used to write the correct answer on a piece of paper that is held up in the air for the instructor to see. Perhaps the most elegant method is the use of personal whiteboards or magnetic fluid boards. The point is that each learner is active in trying to learn, and that makes learning deeper, more meaningful, and more memorable . . . which is why we are teaching in the first place.

## Summary

1   Instructors traditionally love having whole-class discussions because, in that way, they believe they are teaching at high levels. Learners love discussions also, but for different reasons. In whole-class discussions, one person at time speaks, and therefore most learners can sit back and listen—or not.
2   In reality, whole-class discussions are recitations and do not involve the "whole class"

3   Breaking a discussion down into components and assigning those components to small groups is more effective and helps engage all learners.

4   Instructors routinely make common mistakes in asking questions, and avoiding them will improve their instruction.

5   Four corners debates allow learners to choose the answers that they think are the most correct. Then the learners can develop a method to support their thinking.

6   High- and low-tech learner response systems help learners to take the risk of answering a question and help them get immediate feedback on whether they are on target or not. The systems also help the instructor to know at what level each learner is functioning.

## Questions to Consider

1   With my new understanding of whole-class discussions, what is my plan to replace those?

_____

_____

_____

_____

2   Which of the common mistakes do I make, and what am I going to do to correct them?

_____

_____

_____

_____

3   How would I set up a "four corners" debate with the topics my learners are studying now?

Questions

_____

_____

_____

_____

Corner 1

_____

_____

_____

_____

Corner 2

_____

_____

_____

_____

Corner 3

_____

_____

_____

_____

Corner 4

_____

_____

_____

_____

4   What questions do I want to use for individual response where all learn-
    ers respond either in high- or low-tech ways?

    High-tech method:

_____

_____

_____

_____

Low-tech method:

_____

_____

_____

_____

Question Progression:

_____

_____

_____

_____

_____

_____

_____

_____

_____

_____

_____

_____

_____

_____

_____

## 13.4 Physiological Questions: How Do You Engage All Participants' Brains and Bodies With Questions?

### Total Physical Response

Foreign-language instructors know of a methodology that capitalizes on the fact that the body is connected to the brain. They call it "Total Physical

Response."[15] This means that the instructor asks a question in a way that the learners have to physically show they understand the answer, not just give the answer. Whether it is drawing a map of the US in the air and showing where Florida is or miming the procedure to change a tire, TPR gets the body and the mind moving in the right direction. In some ways, TPR is very similar to the game Simon Says and, in fact, I use Simon Says TPR as test to see which learners are struggling (see Chapter 11 for examples of Simon Says questions).

TPR is also an excellent vocabulary-building tool for any classroom, not just foreign language. An instructor can have a lot of fun by being creative in what they ask the learners to do to show they know the answer: the learners can point, touch, stand next to, move, grab, lift, sit on, sit under, stand on, etc. An easy way to start is by simply asking the learners to point to the answer in a book and raise their hand when they have it found it. To cement the learning, they can then share their answers with their partners or groups. The answers you have them interact with can be anywhere. The learners can point to in the book, on the wall, on the board, etc. Word walls, for example, are great for vocabulary building (I use all four walls as word walls), but they are much more powerful if referred to frequently; simply having the words on the wall will not help the learners to learn them. With TPR, by asking them to find the word that means "chemical that allows plants to create energy from the sun" by pointing to it on the wall, an instructor can not only help learners to learn the words, but they will find out immediately which learners don't know what chlorophyll is (they will not point or will point to the wrong location). For struggling learners, TPR activities are an excellent opportunity to learn without being embarrassed. All they have to do is watch what other learners do and mimic them.

Below are some sample WILD HOG Questions for TPR according to Costa's Level of difficulty:

## Costa Level 1 questions

Point to, touch, stand next to, etc.
(Yes or no) Nod or thumbs up/down. . . . Is this ___? Can I ____ with this?
If this is correct, stand up. Raise your hand if you agree.

## Costa Level 2 questions

Take the equation step card given you and line up in an order that makes sense.

Place the sentence cards in the correct order.
Categorize the animals depicted on the slides by genus, then filum, then order.

**Costa Level 3 questions**

Stand under the quote on the wall that best illustrates your understanding of Willa Cather's *My Antonia*.

Go to the corner of the room you think is the best answer posted on the wall to this question: "Jeff has a job that pays $8.00 an hour. He works 20 hours a week. How much money can he save if puts 20% of his earnings in the bank the first month?"

On the walls are posters containing a possible cause of the Great Depression. Choose a poster that best identifies the most likely culprit. Prepare a two-minute statement for your group as to why you chose this as the cause, with supporting evidence.

You will perform a gallery walk and read the statements on the wall. For each statement give your response either in agreement or disagreement with at least one supporting piece of evidence.

Another level of Total Physical Response is telling stories. I mean stories about anything! Any topic or any subject can be made into a story, and, according to Dr. Daniel Willingham, our brains are wired for hearing and telling stories. The creation of these stories is based on questions about protagonists, plot, scenery, climax, and resolution. The telling of the stories uses gestures and actions that help the learners cement the information in their brains. Have you heard the one about the wicked denominator that refused to change in order to marry the beautiful compound fraction?

## Summary

1 Accessing a learner's brain by asking questions that have them move their bodies is called Total Physical Response.
2 TPR is excellent for vocabulary building when used in conjunction with items placed on the four walls of the room.
3 TPR WILD HOG progressions move learning from the lower Costa Level 1 to Level 3.
4 TPR storytelling is another level where the learners will have to ask the story questions to make and tell action stories about anything.

## Questions to Consider

1    How will I use TPR in my current instructional assignment?

_____

_____

_____

_____

2    What question progression can I make to employ TPR at all of Costas's Levels?

_____

_____

_____

_____

Level 1

_____

_____

_____

_____

Level 2

_____

_____

_____

_____

Level 3

_____

_____

_____

_____

3    What are my plans to use TPR storytelling?

_____

_____

_____

_____

## Notes

1  I found several research studies that show that teachers ask up to 150 questions per half-hour, and nearly 80% of those questions are knowledge-based questions or, in other words, cognitively easy questions (Albergaria, 2010; Tienken, Goldberg, & DiRocco, 2009; Sahin & Kulm, 2008; Filippone, 1998).
2  Dossett & Burns, 2000.
3  H. Lyn Erickson is the "godmother" of concept-based curriculum. The idea that concept knowledge transfers but not factual knowledge is foundational to her theories. If learners understand one concept, they can transfer that knowledge or generalize it to other situations. Erickson, H. L., Lanning, L. A., & French, R. (2017). *Concept-based curriculum and instruction for the thinking classroom* (2nd ed.). Corwin a SAGE Publishing Company. ISBN 9781506355399.
4  The effect of cortisol on the brain: Along with the obvious and not-so-obvious student reactions, asking questions to the whole group has some physiological and cognitive implications when a student has to answer in front of the whole group. According to brain researchers, when students are put in situations that could be embarrassing or frightful, a hormone called cortisol is released, and the organ within the brain that is most affected is called the hippocampus. This organ is responsible for cataloguing and retrieving memories. It basically shuts down in the presence of cortisol, and the memory functions of storage and retrieval are inhibited (Caine & Caine, 1991, p. 65; Sylwester, 1995; Willingham, 2010). Exposing one's ignorance to an entire class for some students is enough to trigger the fight or flight mechanisms. Clammy hands, lead feeling in the stomach, dry mouth, and nervous agitation are other physiological manifestations of this phenomenon. During the course of their learning careers, the average student has learned several methods of avoiding this type of confrontation. Because of this, when an instructor decides to go cherry picking for students to answer questions, he may get a few sour ones.

5   Zombie jokes! See https://bestdadjokes.com/zombie-jokes/.

6   Lemov, 2015.

7   Krashen, S. D. (1986). *Principles and practice in second language acquisition*. Oxford: Pergamon Press. Retrieved from www.sdkrashen.com/content/books/principles_and_practice.pdf

8   Varela, Cater, & Michel, 2015.

9   Bruner, 1973; Vygotsky, 1978; Bassano & Christison, 1982; Azmi, 2013.

10  When I spent several days and shadowed the students from class to class, the other thing that I learned was that I got very tired of sitting on those hard, uncomfortable chairs. After short periods of time, I became annoyed at having to listen to teacher after teacher, who like to hear the sound of their own voice. They would just talk and talk and expect the students to soak it in. The hard seats and the continual droning of the teachers made it very hard to pay attention. For a while, I was suffering brain stagnation. I was amazed that the students seemed to handle this better than I did. Perhaps they are more patient than I am or they just expected school to be like that and dealt with it as best they could. Well, I had trouble being patient because I know that school does not have to be like that. I firmly believe that it would do teachers good to sit in their student's places now and then. Every teacher should understand the student perspective and strive to get students to be active learners, primarily by being active teachers.

11  Caine & Caine, 1991; Sylwester, 1995; Zull, 2004; Willingham, 2010. An interesting experiment was performed on London taxi drivers and bus drivers. Each kind of driver had an MRI done to measure the size of their hippocampus. When the information was analyzed, the researchers discovered that the taxi drivers had larger hippocampi than the bus drivers. The reason is due to the nature of their professions. Taxi drivers had to figure out ways to get from point A to point B, and in London this involves some pretty complex thinking. But bus drivers performed the same route from memory every day with little or no thought. You can read the research at www.fil.ion.ucl.ac.uk/Maguire/Maguire2006.pdf.

12  In a refreshingly honest research article about social studies teachers, Dr. William Wilen makes the critical distinction that most of what teachers call classroom discussions are in fact recitations. True discussions, he goes on to explain, are, "oral explorations of ideas, issues, and problems . . . that request new information rather than memorized facts from the text."

13  Schmoker, 2006, p. 55.

14  Marzano, 2007, p. 98.

15 James Asher wrote about Total Physical Response in 1967 primarily to help participants learn foreign languages. If you want to learn more about TPR, check out these websites: www.tpr-world.com/ and www.tprsource.com/. There is also TPRS or Total Physical Response Storytelling, which foreign language teachers use to help students communicate in the target language. See www.tprstories.com/what-is-tprs.

## References

Albergaria, P. (2010). Questioning patterns, questioning profiles and teaching strategies in secondary education. *International Journal of Learning*, *17*(1), 587–600. doi:10.1504/IJLC.2010.035833

Azmi, M. N. L. (2013). National language policy and its impacts on second language reading culture. *Journal of International Education and Leadership*, *3*(1). https://eric.ed.gov/?q=Azmi%2c+2013&id=EJ1136083

Bassano, S. K., & Christison, M. A. (1982). Developing successful conversation groups. *TESL Talk*, *13*(3), 18–27.

Bruner, J. (1973). *The relevance of education*. W.W. Norton & Company. Retrieved from https://books.google.com/books/about/The_Relevance_of_Education.html?id=2aMXJ877HjEC

Caine, R., & Caine, G. (1991). *Making connections: Teaching and the human brain*. Alexandria, VA: Association for Supervision and Curriculum Development.

Dossett, D., & Burns, B. (2000). The development of children's knowledge of attention and resource allocation in single and dual tasks. *The Journal of Genetic Psychology*, *161*(2), 216–234. Retrieved September 5, 2009, from Research Library. (Document ID: 54901844).

Erickson, H. L., Lanning, L. A., & French, R. (2017). *Concept-based curriculum and instruction for the thinking classroom* (2nd ed.). Corwin a SAGE Publishing Company. ISBN 9781506355399

Filippone, M. (1998). *Questioning at the elementary level* (pp. 417–431). Washington, DC: ERIC.

Krashen, S. D. (1986). *Principles and practice in second language acquisition*. Oxford: Pergamon Press.

Lemov, D. (2015). *Teach like a champion 2.0*. San Francisco, CA: Wiley.

Marzano, R. (2007). *The art and science of teaching: A comprehensive framework for effective instruction*. Alexandria, VA: Association for Supervision and Curriculum Development.

Sahin, A., & Kulm, G. (2008). Sixth grade mathematics teachers' intension and use of probing, guiding, and factual questions. *Journal of Math Teacher Education*, *2008*(11), 221–241. https://doi.org/10.1007/s10857-008-9071-2

Schmoker, M. (2006). *Results now: How we can achieve unprecedented improvements in teaching and learning*. Alexandria, VA: Association for Supervision and Curriculum Development.

Sylwester, R. (1995). *A celebration of neurons: An educator's guide to the human brain*. Alexandria, VA: Association for Supervision and Curriculum Development.

Tienken, C. H., Goldberg, S., & DiRocco, D. (2009). Questioning the questions. *Kappa Delta Pi Record*, 46(1), 39–43. Retrieved December 12, 2011, from https://search.ebscohost.com/login.aspx?direct=true&db=ehh&AN=45 422447&site=eds-live

Varela, O. E., Cater III, J. J., & Michel, N. (2015). Learner-instructor similarity: A social attribution approach to learning. *Journal of Management Development*, 34(4), 460.

Vygotsky, L. S. (1978). *Zone of proximal development: A new approach, mind in society*. Cambridge, MA: Harvard University Press.

Willingham, D. (2010). *Why don't students like school*. San Francisco, CA: Jossey-Bass.

Zull, J. E. (2004). The art of changing the brain. *Education Leadership*, 62, 68–72.

# 14

## Accountable Talk

### How Do You Help Participants to
### Support Their Answers?

Chapter 5, "Substantiveness," discusses the idea of being rigorous in the questions and the answers. Modeling rigor includes citing sources and employing a progression of questions that leads to Costa's Level 3, Bloom's Creation (problem solving, evaluation), and Erickson's knowledge level of Theory.

## 14.1 Question Training: How Can Participants Learn to Ask Effective Questions?

### Difference Between Instruction and Training

When I did some training for the US ARMY Medical Training Hospital in San Antonio, Texas, I learned some distinctions between the words "educate" and "train." In order truly to describe the difference, I need to tell you a story. This story was related to me by the of dean of the school. The ARMY Medical Training School prepares EMTs and other medical personnel to operate in the field. In one EMT class, the soldiers learned how to stage a triage as wounded from a battle come into the medical section. The soldiers were trained to evaluate each patient and perform initial life-saving first aid as necessary, then go on to the next patient. In order to save on bandages and medical supplies, the soldiers were trained to not open the bandage package but simply to tape it on over the wound. One by one the soldiers pretending to be wounded were evaluated by the medical officer being trained and as necessary received a package of bandages taped to the claimed injury. This drill was repeated over and over until the medical officers could do it quickly and effortlessly. This group of medical EMTs graduated and went out into the field of combat. One of the medical EMTs was assigned to an active combat situation and was faced with establishing a triage. He did exactly what he was trained to do. He evaluated every patient and those who needed immediate medical attention, and to the chagrin of his commanding officer, this EMT dutifully taped unopened bandage packages over the wounds of each patient. With this story as a backdrop, the idea of training is making actions so ingrained that they do not require thought. Education, on the other hand, is the ability to think out a situation and then determine the best course of action. Just as in the military, we want learners trained to respond to certain situations (correctly) without having to think about it. In other situations, we want the learners to use their higher-order thinking skills to make decisions and create solutions.

## Training Learners to Ask Questions

The training has much to do with behavioral psychology. When a stimulus is given, we want an autonomous response. For example, through repetition we have trained our learners that, if they want to answer a question, they raise their hand. Some instructors require learners to answer the questions with completed sentences. Others require their learners to stand when they have been called on to answer a question. We can and should train learners not only on how to answer questions but also how to ask them correctly. Throughout this entire book I have been helping you to refine your ability to ask questions. Now, it is your turn to help your learners refine their ability to ask questions by training them to do it automatically, as a habit[1]. Multiple research studies—and common sense—show that, when a learner is asking questions, real learning is taking place.[2] But getting learners to that point takes a bit of preparation (see Section 14.1).

Be brave, because as soon as you do train your learners in the three levels of questions from Arthur Costa, they will start judging your questions. You might even want them to evaluate your questions, and when your questions are sub-par then they should feel free to point that out to you. Often the question is more important than the answer, as any real scientist will tell you. Not that answers are not important, but, given the right question, many doors of inquiry may be opened. How do you get your learners to ask great questions? You train them until it is a habit.

*You can tell whether a man is clever by his answers. You can tell whether a man is wise by his questions.*
—*Naguib Mahfouz, 1988 Nobel Prize for Literature*

### Developing Habits of Mind

You may want to disagree with me, but I believe that humans are creatures of habit. Even more than that, we could not survive without habits. Everything about us is habitual, from the foot we put our sock on first to how we brush our teeth. But it even goes deeper than that. Not only do we have physical, muscle-memory habits, we also have emotional habits and even mental habits, a well-worn track that our mind has followed many times. You've all heard the 21-days-in-a-row bunk about developing habits.[3] It is different for every person and for every situation. Some can be less; other habits take longer than 21 days. Malcom Gladwell claimed that 10,000 hours of doing something makes you an expert, why?[4] Because now you are trained to do it, and it becomes a habit (see Table 14.1). Our learners deserve to know how to question and think critically, but they won't unless we consistently train them to do it. It needs to be habitual for them to challenge what they hear, what they read, and what they see. The only way that happens is if instructors consistently allow them to use their questioning skills in their current studies. Instructors, as has been mentioned several times in this book, need to create a learning environment where it is OK to disagree and back up thoughts with evidence.

## 14.2 Socratic Questions: Answering Questions With Questions

Perhaps I have used Socrates as an example too often because I am proposing a different learning model. Rather than envisioning a phenomenal questioner, like Socrates[5] firing brain-throbbing questions to a room full of eagerly but passively listening learners, I would like to replace that vision with the vision

Table 14.1 Developing Questioning Habits in Learners

| Learner Questioning Habits to Develop: |
| --- |
| ◆ Use divergent questions, not so many convergent |
| ◆ Limit closed "yes-/no" or "true/false" |
| ◆ Limit double-barreled questions—use of "and/or" |
| ◆ Use progressive levels of questions—123—Costa |
| ◆ Prepare your questions in advance (WILD HOG) |
| ◆ Avoid leading questions |
| ◆ Be prepared to provide citations to support your question |

**Table 14.2** Categories of Socratic Questions

| Types of Socratic Questions | |
| --- | --- |
| Probing Questions | Getting more and deeper |
| Verifying Questions | Restating in different words. |
| Challenging Assumptions and Biases | Requesting evidence |
| Process Questions | If then, what's next |
| Propositional Questions | What if |
| Opinion Questions | How do you feel vs think |
| Contrasting Questions | Opposites, devil's advocate. |

of a physical or virtual room full of eager learners who each have a series of brain-throbbing questions to ask their partners concerning a topic they have studied. Later we will explore some of the types of questions that these eager learners might be asking each other. Given the ability to ask Socratic questions, your learners will want to engage in debate with their partners, small groups, debate teams, caucus groups, and the whole class. Trying to engage the learners will not be an issue. If you are interested, as I was, in seeing what is out there about "types of questions," you may be as disappointed, as I was, in finding that there is no agreement on types of questions, and the examples given for proposed types of questions are contrived and don't even match their "proposed" question classifications. So, I did what seems to make sense to me—and hopefully to you. I made my own classifications so that you can share them with your learners (see Table 14.2).

## Probing Questions

One of the things that I took to heart when I was an online instructor for the University of Phoenix teacher preparation program was the idea of making sure the answer to the question was substantive. I learned rather quickly that, in order to get substantive answers, I had to ask question of my learners that would elicit substantive answers. If I did not get a substantive answer, then I had to use probing questions to get to substantiveness. In other words, I did not accept generic answers or answers that were obviously superficial or incomplete. The probing questions are meant to get more out of the learner, get them to explain themselves more clearly, and motivate them to help us understand what they are referring too. It could be asking them to define a word they used or elucidate more on a particular reference to which they alluded. Some would call this clarifying, but I put this under probing for more information. Please remember that a question is a request for information, whether in question format or statement format. For example:

"Tell me more please."

"I don't understand. Please explain more."

"When you used the word 'Etruscan,'[6] what did you mean?"

"Please explain what you meant by 'too much'."

"To which part of a computer were you referring?"

"Shakespeare made many philosophical statements, to which were you alluding?"

## Verifying Questions

When I learned how to be an educational leadership coach, one of the concepts that was drilled into myself and the other participants in the training was the Steven R. Covey 5th[7] habit, seek first to understand before seeking to be understood. The main tool for doing this was to restate or verify your understanding of what the other person has said or written in your own words. This can simply be repeating back the same concepts presented by the other person, or this could also mean reading between the lines and shedding light on what you think the person is really trying to say.

For example:

"If I understand you correctly, you were saying that you believe that Santa Claus is real?"

"Is it true, then that you believe that circle can also be a sphere?"

"From what you stated, you predict that after 2025 money will be all electronic?"

"While you stated that you hated *The Scarlet Letter* by Nathaniel Hawthorne, what you are really saying is that you would prefer to read something that relates more to today. Am I correct?"

## Challenging Assumptions and Biases

We all make decisions and base our opinions on assumptions and our personal biases. The act of revealing those is called disclosure, and few individuals are willing to do that. Effective questioning can reveal those biases. For this reason, we have the practice in our courts of allowing cross examination.

For example:

"How would you describe your personal beliefs on the topic of prayer in schools?"

"With which elements of the idea of suzerainty do you disagree?"

"Why do you prefer chocolate ice cream to strawberry ice cream?"

## Process Questions

Identifying the way things are done is often as important as knowing why they are done. Each step in a process often signifies a juncture where a choice or decision was made. Following the process identifies those intermediate decisions that led to the final conclusion. No academic endeavor is void of procedures and process; whether it is an algebraic equation's step-by-step resolution or the deliberate accumulation of evidence in the construction of a persuasive essay, the steps that are taken deserve to be analyzed and questioned. The intent of process questions is to identify a pivotal point that contributed to the success or failure of the entire process or that planted the seeds of success or failure for the entire project.

For example:

"Please explain to me the steps you took to arrive at this conclusion. How did you get from here to there?"

"Which procedure contributed most toward the final objective?"

"In your experiment, at what point did you determine that something went wrong?"

"In dealing with other teams of professionals, what was your key to success?"

"In the presidential election of 1860, what factors influenced the outcome?"

## Propositional Questions

Propositional questions are often referred to as "what if" questions. These questions also ask for predictions and possible outcomes based on factual or hypothetical situations. The whole idea behind these questions is to remove current restrictions and obstacles and, within that new freedom, ask, "How would things be different?" The intent is to draw opinions, beliefs, and aspirations out of the person or people being questioned. These questions take several forms such as, "If you had a magic wand . . .", "If money were no object . . .", "If you were the president . . .", "What do you think happened when . . . ?", or "If you could change anything . . ." They tend to be personalized and induce often whimsical and sometime poignant answers.

For example:

"If there were no law against vandalism, what would be the consequences?"

"How would you write the last chapter of *To Kill a Mockingbird*?"

"If you were an alien, what would you think about schools?"

"If I gave you a million dollars, what would you do with it?"

"How would John Steinbeck's *The Pearl*, end differently if he viewed human nature as more kind?"

"Upon reflecting on the results of this project, what could you have done differently?"

## Opinion Questions

Opinion questions can be asked directly: "What is your opinion?" or indirectly, leaving out the words "think," "opinion," or "feel," but in both situations they request the person or people to respond with what they think or feel. Appealing to the thought processes is what we would normally categorize as opinion, but, as you may have discovered in your dealings with other humans, often "opinion" may have little to do with what a person thinks and much more to do with what that person feels. Advertising understands this concept so completely that, in order to sell something, especially a large ticket item such as a vehicle, they will appeal to the customer's emotions rather than their brains. They show pictures of elegant women and handsome men enjoying themselves. They show video clips of a sparkly car careening around a curve in a beautiful mountain pass. Rarely will they show the specs of the car before they show you the leather seats and fancy interior. In these types of questions, the words "think" and "feel" are often interchanged to mean the same thing.

For example:

"When you think about the Venezuelan economic crisis, what possible causes come to mind?"

"What do you feel is the best response to an angry customer?"

"What advice would you give to a programmer feeling pressure to complete a project but wanting to spend more time with his family?"

"What is your opinion about Roe vs. Wade?"

"How do you think that you could have handled this situation better?"

"What is the most important thing to consider in building a home?"

## Contrasting Questions

Contrasting questions are just that. They ask the opposite of the topic and are meant to identify flaws in thinking. In contradicting, many label this as taking the "devil's advocate" position, though care must be taken in using this title when issues concerning right and wrong or moral concerns are discussed.

For example:

"If I take light as the opposite of darkness, then what is the opposite of illumination?"

"When electricity is introduced in water, hydrogen and oxygen are produced. How do you do the reverse?"

"How did the notion that the world was flat affect explorers? How are we different today?"

"If censorship is the correct response, who decides what gets censored and what doesn't?"

"Please explain why solar power is not the future of energy production."

"What question wasn't asked?"

"What was the real intent or meaning?"

## 14.3  Logic

Questions that use logic abound, especially if you want to trick test takers. Delimiters—"all," "most," "some," "one," "none"—can make questions more difficult and more complex. As earlier stated, this kind of question does not happen on the fly. This is something that you have to WILD HOG, i.e. write in advance. The use of the logical operators "And," "Or," "Xor (Exclusive Or)," etc. is discussed in Chapter 5.

### Syllogisms

How are syllogistic questions created? You provide two pieces of information and then ask the learner to consider the third. For example:

A dog has four legs, and an animal that has four legs travels on land, therefore dogs travel on land.

The question would be, if a dog has four legs and animals that have four legs travel on land, then what else can we say about dogs? To provide more difficulty, you can do a reverse syllogistic question (usually they don't work like this one). Example:

If dogs travel on land, and animals that have four legs travel on land, what else can we say about dogs?

How can we change the syllogism so that it works?

## 14.4  Inquiry Learning: How Can Participants Use Questions to Learn?

When I was the program manager for grant funded by the Ford Fund,[8] I witnessed firsthand the transformation that can take place when learners are given the reins of learning. I gathered 26 ninth-grade participants from three different school districts in San Antonio to participate in the Ford Partnerships for Advanced Studies (Ford PAS) program. I vividly remember the first session. These young participants were placed in groups of five and one of six and given a design task and set loose. They just sat there. None of them had a clue as to what to do next. By encouraging them and giving them advice, they began their learning journey. Every learning activity they did was designed to get them to work together to ask questions and resolve issues. These young people learned to jump in with both feet and ask the hard questions, plan, fail, and retry until success was reached. Their last project was to devise three tests to show the strength of different types of plastic in order to choose the best one for their product. The videos of their results showing unique and effective testing processes were amazing. After six weeks of inquiry learning, these learners had transformed from being timid and unimaginative into curious, ambitious, and brave learners. This is the power of inquiry learning.[9]

### Curiosity

The point of inquiry learning is that the end result is not known by anyone. The instructor has a general idea of what might come from the activity and definitely has an idea of what learning will take place in order to complete the project, but the direction of the learning all depends on the questions (inquiry) that are generated by the learners. Getting learners to start asking the questions means that the instructor must set the stage beforehand by creating a "relevant-to-the-learner" scenario; an issue to resolve or a need to fill. Then create the boundaries of the learning activity in terms of time and expected outcomes. Finally, the instructor gives the learners all the information and tools they need, gets out of the way, and lets them start to work. The phases of inquiry learning can be summed up in the Scientific Five E model[10] (see Figure 14.1 and Table 14.3): Engage, Explore, Explain, Extend, and Evaluate.

**Across:**

    1 Extend: what do learners do to dig deeper for more understanding?
    4 Explain: how do learners communicate their understanding?
    5 Engage: what do learners do to begin their learning investigations?

## Inquiry Learning Five E Model

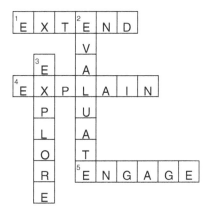

**Figure 14.1** The Five E Inquiry Model

**Down**[11]:

2 Evaluate: how do learners verify their understanding and determine the success of their inquiry?
3 Explore: what do learners do to observe carefully and look for understanding?

## Summary

1 Training is different than educating. In training we do not want "thinking" but quick automatic responses.
2 Training learners to ask their own questions means that they will be able to evaluate your questions as well. Training means that they develop habits of mind, and automatically their brains go to correct questioning habits.
3 Socrates never answered a question without giving a question. When we speak of Socratic questions, we are talking about questions that clarify, probe, challenge, and extend knowledge.
4 Inquiry means asking questions because you don't know the answers, not even as the instructor.
5 If learners use questions to investigate or inquire, they develop their observational power and their curiosity.
6 Inquiry learning means that, once given the parameters of inquiry or problem that needs to be investigated or solved, the learners are in charge, and the instructor is an observer and coach.

Table 14.3 Five E Inquiry Questions for Learners

| Engage | Explore | Experiment | Explain | Extend |
|---|---|---|---|---|
| • Issue Questions | • Observation Questions | • Process Questions | • Documentation Questions | • Findings Questions |
| • What is the issue? | • What am I looking at? | • What questions do I have? | • What documentation can I create to show the data? | • How does the data predict future behaviors? |
| • Why is it important? | • How can I describe it? | • How can I find out more information? | | • What patterns emerge from the data? |
| • How does it affect me? | • What are the pieces? | • What kind of experiment can I perform? | • What is the relationship between the data and the documentation? | • What applications are there to use this data? |
| • What am I interested in? | • How does it work? | | | • Evaluation Questions |
| • What do I already know? | • What are the rules? | • How do I isolate what I want to know? | • What kind of visuals do I need to use to best explain? | • How can I verify my conclusions? |
| • What tools do I have? | • What is the process? | • What variables can I control? | | • What measurement can I use to gauge progress? |
| • Where do I start? | • What happens when I change something? | • What variable can I not control? | • How much data do I need to show? | • Reflection Questions |
| • How far do I go? | • What happens in different conditions or circumstances? | • Attention to Detail Questions | • Data Analysis Questions | • What successes did I experience? |
| • How do I know when I am done? | • What or whom does this affect? | • What details stand out? | • What does the data show? | • How can I improve the process the next time? |
| • How will I know when I am successful? | • How does this relate to what I know? | • What is missing? | • What does the data suggest? | • What obstacles can I avoid? |
| • What are my time constraints? | | • What is unique? | | • What extra assistance did I need? |
| | | • What are the outliers? | | • What was the greatest thing I learned? |
| | | • How can others do the same experiment? | | |

## Questions to Consider

1    What training will I provide to my learners to help them to ask effective questions?

_____

_____

_____

2    Relevant to my current instruction, how would I write the following Socratic questions?

_____

_____

_____

Probing Questions:

_____

_____

_____

Verifying Questions:

_____

_____

_____

Challenging Assumptions Questions:

_____

_____

_____

Process Questions:

_____

_____

_____

Opinion Questions:

_____

_____

_____

Contrasting Questions:

_____

_____

_____

3  What kind of preparation do I need to inspire my learners to practice inquiry?

_____

_____

_____

4  What kind of inquiry questions should I train my learners to ask?

_____

_____

_____

5  How do I develop curiosity in my learners?

_____

_____

_____

## Notes

1  From one of my colleagues at Edutopia, Heather Wolpert-Gawron, Stirring Students to Ask Tougher Questions retrieved from: www.edutopia. org/costa-questioning-levels-wolpert-gawron
2  Here are two studies about students asking questions: Bauer, H. H., & Snizek, W. E. (1989). Encouraging students in large classes to ask questions: Some promising results from classes in chemistry and sociology. *Teaching Sociology, 17*(3), 337–340. https://doi.org/10.2307/1318081; Zeegers, Y., & Elliott, K. (2019). Who's asking the questions in classrooms? Exploring teacher practice and student engagement in generating engaging and intellectually challenging questions. *Pedagogies, 14*(1), 17–32. https://doi.org/10.1080/1554480X.2018.1537186
3  Itzchakov, G., Uziel, L., & Wood, W. (2018). When attitudes and habits don't correspond: Self-control depletion increases persuasion but not behavior. *Journal of Experimental Social Psychology, 75*, 1–10. https://doi.

org/10.1016/j.jesp.2017.10.011. See also www.psychologytoday.com/us/blog/brain-wise/201904/the-science-habits

4 *Outliers* (2008), www.gladwellbooks.com/.

5 Socrates never wrote anything. It was his students and observers who wrote what he said.

6 The Estrucans lived 600 years BC between the Tiber and Arno rivers of Italy. Some say they are the ancestors of the first Italians. They fought the Greeks and the Romans, then the Romans assimilated them. www.britannica.com/topic/Etruscan

7 If you need a wonderful refresher of the Seven Habits (Covey, 1989), I found this two-part video series from Wisdom for Life helpful: www.youtube.com/watch?v=WFc08j9eorQ

8 What used to be called the Ford Partnerships for Advanced Studies (PAS) is now call Ford Next Generation Learning (NGL). It is an inquiry-based program that mixes business and stem and teaches creative problem solving. https://fordngl.com/

9 Here is an article I wrote regarding inquiry: www.edutopia.org/blog/redefining-failure-ben-johnson

10 Bennett, Colette. "What Is the 5 E Instructional Model?" ThoughtCo, Aug. 28, 2020, thoughtco.com/5-e-instructional-model-4628150. You can also see the source by Bybee, Rodger W., et al. "The BSCS 5 E Instructional Model: Origins and Effectiveness." A report prepared for the Office of Science Education, National Institutes of Health.

11 Easy and free crossword makers: https://pdf.theteacherscorner.net/file_viewer.php, www.education.com/worksheet-generator/reading/crossword-puzzle/, www.puzzle-maker.com/crossword_Design.cgi, www.edu-games.org/word-games/crosswords/crossword-maker.php and many more. These are free for at least one crossword, some never charge, and others cost from the beginning.

## References

Bauer, H. H., & Snizek, W. E. (1989). Encouraging students in large classes to ask questions: Some promising results from classes in chemistry and sociology. *Teaching Sociology, 17*(3), 337–340. https://doi.org/10.2307/1318081

Bennett, C. (2020, August 28). What is the 5 e instructional model? *ThoughtCo*. Retrieved December 2020, from http:///thoughtco.com/5-e-instructional-model-4628150

Covey, S. (1989). *Seven habits of highly effective people*. New York: Simon & Schuster.

Gladwell, M. (2008). *Outliers: The story of success*. New York: Little, Brown and Company.

Itzchakov, G., Uziel, L., & Wood, W. (2018). When attitudes and habits don't correspond: Self-control depletion increases persuasion but not behavior. *Journal of Experimental Social Psychology*, *75*, 1–10. https://doi.org/10.1016/j.jesp.2017.10.011

Zeegers, Y., & Elliott, K. (2019). Who's asking the questions in classrooms? Exploring teacher practice and student engagement in generating engaging and intellectually challenging questions. *Pedagogies*, *14*(1), 17–32. https://doi.org/10.1080/1554480X.2018.1537186

# 15

## Controlling Questions

### How Do You Use Questions to Manage the Class?

To create an atmosphere of learning, as discussed in Section 8.4, showing encouragement and positive regard in your attempt to inspire learning is essential. The questions must also place the responsibility for learning squarely on the shoulders of the participants and place you in the role of resource and coach. Managing the classroom has three elements 1) Anticipating and eliminating possible time-wasters: inefficiencies, misunderstandings, and discipline issues prior to the lesson; 2) implementing effective processes and high-performance attitudes while dealing with issues as they arise; 3) redirecting unproductive behaviors. As the instructor consistently uses these ownership-style questions, not only will they create a safe, productive learning environment by modifying and channeling unproductive behaviors into positive paths, but the instructor will also find that these unproductive behaviors will be eliminated before they start.

See Figure 15.1 for possible questions for each category.

### Taking-Responsibility Questions

When learners take responsibility for their learning, it is helpful to guide them in their thinking so they can not only feel like they are in charge but they can also learn how to actively and aggressively pursue learning independently (see Figure 15.2).

## 15.1 Survey Questions: What Do You Know About Your Participants' Thinking?

Getting to know what participants are really thinking could be the topic of a series of "how-to" books, so I am only going to get you started on some

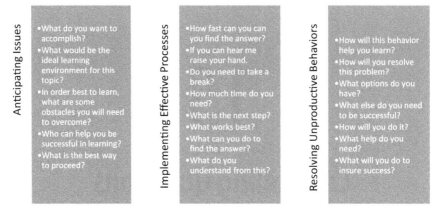

**Figure 15.1** Questions to Motivate Learners

**Figure 15.2** Questions to Empower Learner Responsibility

ideas of what you can do. The following are some traditional and nontraditional methods for taking a dipstick measurement of where your learners are. Make sure you consider your audience and how they may respond to the information gathering. For learners in K–12, make sure the in-class polls do not require protected information such as religious beliefs, cultural or racial groups, political affiliation, or economic status. Most school districts have policies that all research surveys and polls be approved through the principal first. Make sure the topic of the inquiry and answers are appropriate as a part of your instructions. Of course, for ultimate engagement, have your participants create the instrument and/or have them administer it. Be prepared to deal with outliers: learners who wish to make a statement with their answers, be humorous, or overly critical. Finally, these forms of inquiry are great for obtaining data for learners to gather, graph, and analyze.

Avoid creating questions that are leading, insinuating, double-barreled, or confusing. If you recall, in Section 8.3, the idea of leading questions was used to help learners arrive at the most correct answer. In surveying, however, the question must not lead the respondent to a particular answer; if so, the survey results will not be valid (example: how much did you enjoy the wonderful presentation on customer service?). Survey questions that represent your particular biases must also be avoided (example: how successful are you at eliminating the stench of plagiarism in your papers?). Double-barreled questions are two-part questions and should be separated to make two questions instead of one (example: do you believe that the second amendment is valid, and would you agree that guns should be registered?). When the answer choices are too similar or redundant, i.e. are the same, just stated in different words, it makes it difficult for the respondent to answer, invalidating the responses (example: what is your preferred electronic tool? (A. Tablet, B. iPhone, C. Smartphone, D. Laptop).

## 15.2 Polls

Instantaneous polls can be taken simply by asking: "How well do you think you have mastered this topic?" The responses could be thumbs up, sideways, or down, or if you fully understand the topic go to this corner, so-so that corner, and if you feel you need more help come over here with me. If you would like something more concrete, you can use smartphones, tablets, and laptops to take a pulse of what your participants are thinking: Kahoot, Poll Everywhere, PollDaddy, Micropoll, Zeetings.[1] Aside from these applications, if you use Google Classroom or maybe your LMS, you can create poll buttons for participants to respond to.

## 15.3 Surveys and Questionnaires

Surveys are not only the questionnaires but also include the delivery and analysis of the responses. Surveys create a data trend by sampling a small portion of the population. Typically, surveys with fewer than 100 respondents are not considered valid. To be technical, because of the small numbers in a typical learning group, all of the learners usually receive a questionnaire, which, in fact, makes it a census (surveying the entire population). In creating effective questionnaires—or lists of questions—for learning, remember the advice at the beginning of this section. It helps to keep the questionnaires focused on one topic and, for time consideration, keep them short—no more than 15 questions. We are not psychometricians and do not need to do double-blind questionnaires by asking the same questions in different ways. Keep them straightforward and direct. When creating a Likert scale, make sure you clearly label what "1" vs "5" means (1 worst, 5 best, etc.) You also will want an odd number, otherwise there is no middle ground. There are many online survey tools: LimeSurvey, SurveyMonkey, Zoho, and more.[2] Don't forget that your LMS, your institution website, or Google Forms can also provide survey tools for you to use.

## Summary

1   One of the things that we need to make sure happens is that in all cases we reinforce with our questions that learners are responsible for their behavior and how much they learn. This is reflected in the questions we ask regarding their behavior. The monkey is on their shoulders, not ours.

2   Finding out about what and how much your learners know is a wonderful way to customize their learning. Use polls, surveys, and questionnaires to allow you to check for understanding in ways that tell you about each learner and also provide feedback and learning opportunities for your learners.

## Questions to Consider

1   How will I use polls and surveys to check my learners' understanding with what they are learning right now?

_____

_____

_____

Poll Questions:

_____

_____

_____

Survey Questions:

_____

_____

_____

2    How will I adjust the lesson to accommodate for the data obtained?

_____

_____

_____

## Notes

1    For more polling options, see also www.educatorstechnology.com/2018/
      02/17-of-best-surveys-and-polls-creation.html
2    The only one I have found that is completely free without limits is Lime-
      Survey. All the rest have a restricted free version that allow you so many
      surveys to so many people, etc. Here is an article that explains some:
      www.wordstream.com/blog/ws/2014/11/10/best-online-survey-tools.

# Section III

## Learning Conclusion

In this section you delved into the mechanics of asking questions that have already been created (WILD HOG). You learned how to use the brain to greatest effect with Taxon and Locale memory systems. You learned how to ask effective questions that don't turn your learners into zombies. You now know how to avoid common questioning mistakes, especially the whole-class discussion. You learned how to prepare you learners to answer and ask effective questions of their own. Some common threads throughout this section are: questions must be prepared in advance, every learner must be engaged with every question, and the responsibility for learning rests solely on the participants' shoulders. Take a few minutes and create your plan to implement what you have learned so they become "habits of mind" for you. Don't forget to look at the end notes for each chapter for additional sources of learning that you may want to include in your plan.

Section III  Learning Professional Growth Plan

| Professional Growth Activity | Resources Needed | Due Date |
|---|---|---|
| 1. The Role of Repetition in Questions | | |
| | | |
| | | |

| Professional Growth Activity | Resources Needed | Due Date |
|---|---|---|
| 2. Avoiding Zombie Questions | | |
| | | |
| | | |
| 3. Accountable Talk | | |
| | | |
| | | |
| 4. Controlling Questions | | |
| | | |
| | | |
| | | |
| | | |

# Section IV

## Assessing Learning

Sometimes we forget . . . yes, even veteran instructors forget, that we are in the business of alignment.[1] Ah ha! Weren't expecting that one, were you! You thought I was going to say education or teaching people, not content. Well, let me explain why I said alignment. Intellectually, all of us believe in aligning our teaching strategies with the learning needs of each of the learners. We hold that up as the pinnacle of our profession, and we are always searching for ways to reach each and every learner. Yes, we do! But then we are faced with the reality of the classroom situations. We are faced with the question, "How can we align our teaching to 30 different learners or 160 learners?"[2] Effective use of questions can help! (Also see Chapter 7 on differentiation.)

The largest challenge for educators today is to align what we *know* about participant learning with what we actually *do* about participant learning (or what we do to make learning happen).[3] While we certainly make an effort, we still do not do enough alignment of "how we teach" with "how humans learn best." For example, class discussions are prevalent in most classrooms, but, given what you now know about how participants learn and how they respond, leading a typical classroom "discussion" may be a waste of time and energy for two reasons: not all learners participate, and what we call "discussion" is actually a recitation of what the participants are supposed to know (see Section 13.3). Instructors are tempted to believe that they are actually "teaching" when they are engaging learners in a class "discussion" by asking a series of poignant questions designed to lead them to a certain way of thinking (convergent). The real question is, "Are they learning?" We use questions to find out if they are.

# 16

## Checking for Understanding

### How Do You Know All of Your Participants Are Learning?

Let's say you start the class off by asking a review question, "What do Louis Pasteur and Alessandro Volta have in common?" Three students in the front of the class shoot their hands in the air, frantically waving them. Other students are looking at you, politely interested but not raising their hands. You notice a few other students in the back not even looking at you, just doodling in their notepads and, as far as they are concerned, you could have been asking about John the Baptist and Kermit the Frog.[1]

Added to the deluge of sensory information the students in the back are constantly dealing with (remember the reticular formation in Section 2.4?), they are also deluged with thoughts going on inside the brain, such as: "I wish the clowns in front would just grow up! They always want attention", "That was a stupid question! The teacher thinks he's a comedian!", "I can't wait till this class is over! I hate science!" (It is no wonder that students find it hard to pay attention in class!)

Rather than pick on one of the students frantically waving their hands, you choose a girl who, for all intents and purposes, is not paying attention, "Sandra, do you know the answer?"

"Answer to what?" she responds.

"The question I just asked," you say between gritted teeth, because you know that she is baiting you.

"Would you repeat the question please?" she sweetly replies.

You can play this game just as well as she can, "Jim, could you tell Sandra what the question was?"

Jim feels uncomfortable about being a pawn in this battle of wills, but dutifully repeats the question.

"I don't know." Sandra flatly states.

As a professional, you hold your tongue, pause, and then, rather than berate Sandra for not listening and, even worse, not caring about your question, you ask one of the girls in the front that is still waving her hand frantically, "Rachel, what is the answer?"

This review session would have been 100% different if the instructor had simply stated, "Turn to your assigned partner and ask and answer the following ten questions on the whiteboard. I will be circling and checking your progress. After five minutes, you will choose a partner to give the answer you discussed. Ready, go!" In the same space of time, every learner participated, and ten questions were reviewed instead of one.

## 16.1  Checking for Understanding at the End of a Topic

Question: shouldn't instructors check for understanding at the end of every topic?

Answer: no, because you should be constantly checking for understanding and, yes, at least check for understanding the end of a topic. Unfortunately, checking for understanding only at the end of the topic may be a signal to the participants that you are moving on to another subject, and our learners will not really listen to the question but will be waiting for the next topic.

After we have taught a principle or concept, we often ask, "Does everybody understand?" Even though this is primarily a rhetorical question that we really do not expect the learners to answer, we still ask it. What we have to realize is that the participants who do not answer—or even the learners who are nodding their heads up and down answering in the affirmative—may not really understand. Are we aware of how many times we ask this useless question during a day of instruction?

What we really end up telling the students when we ask "Does everyone understand?" or "Are there any questions?" is completely different from what we intend for them to understand. Translated, we in fact are stating:

> OK. Here is your last chance. If you don't ask any questions, then that means that you understand completely, and that I am free to go on to the next subject. Additionally, because I asked this fair question, and I gave you a fair chance to answer, I am absolved from any lack of understanding on your part. I will be able to say in good conscience that I taught you. If you failed to learn it, then it is not my fault!

The fallacy with this thinking is that sometimes the participants do not understand that they do not understand, and if they do not know what they do not know, there is no way that they can ask a question about it. How did Socrates put it? "I know that all I know is that I do not know anything."

The other element to this question is that it is a simple yes-or-no question. Learners will simply say what they think we want to hear. They can tell that we are on a timeline and need to move on, so they will accommodate us, whether they understand or not. Also, participants know that if they really do ask questions, that they might spend another 20 minutes listening to us explaining what we mean. Finally, answering yes-or-no questions does not really give the instructor any useable information and does not push the learners into the higher-order-thinking stratosphere. It is simply too easy to guess. Therefore, asking, "Does everyone understand?" or "Are there any questions?" is never an appropriate method to use for checking for understanding.

There is an easy fix for this. Simply ask, "Thumbs up if you get it, sideways if you sort of get it, thumbs down if you don't get it." Or, "Tell your elbow partner what you understand about. . . . Now ask your partner one question to check to see if they understand."

In Section 13.5, we discuss having your learners show learning by moving their bodies. In Chapter 15, we discuss how using polls, surveys, and technology can give the instructor information on what the learners know and don't know. So, do you have any questions? Good! Let's move on. (I'm joking!)

## 16.2  WILD HOG Questions to Check for Understanding Help the Instructor and the Learner

Question: since the instructor asks the questions and knows the range of acceptable responses, doesn't checking for understanding benefit the instructor more than the learner?

Answer: not entirely. Checking for understanding also helps the learner to identify gaps in knowledge and understanding. If instructors are serious about checking to see how much learners really understand, they have to plan effective WILD HOG Questions that engage every learner and allow multiple opportunities for each learner to grasp the concepts (Rule of Three).

Using WILD HOG Questions helps us to ask specific, open-ended questions rather than simple yes-or-no or short-answer questions to check what they understand. With well-developed progressions of questions, learners can't guess the right answer easily, and they are forced to reveal their current understanding in their answer (i.e. they cannot bluff the instructor into moving on with instruction).

> Bad example: "Did the white rabbit in *Alice in Wonderland* represent something else?"
> (Obviously, yes is the answer, but it does not reveal what the learner knows.)
> Good example: "Talk to your partner and ask, 'What could the words, "I'm late," the oversized pocket watch, and the general nervousness of the white rabbit in *Alice in Wonderland* mean?'"
> Bad example: "What do you understand about stoichiometry?"
> ("What am I supposed to 'understand'?" would be a possible unspoken reply.)
> Good example: "How could you describe stoichiometry to someone who is not familiar with chemistry? You have two minutes to discuss with your partner how you would do this."

Often it is not that the structure of the question is bad, it is the purpose of asking the question *that is in question* (sorry, I couldn't help it) or inappropriate. When questions are *Written Intentionally for Learning Depth and Higher-Order Genius*, (remember the creation of WILD HOG Questions in Chapter 6?), such errors in question construction are fixed because the questions are written and analyzed before instruction begins. Because the thought process before instruction allows us to write great questions, some follow-up questions for the partners could be, "How do scientists use stoichiometry in the lab?", "What can you find out by using stoichiometry?", and "What are the steps for using stoichiometric methods in the classroom?"[2]

## Dealing With Unanswered Questions

What do instructors do when a learner does not know the answer? While this could be viewed by some as a failure on the part of the instructor and the learner, this is actually a learning opportunity (remember Sandra at the beginning of this chapter?). Remember, in a non-WILD HOG Questioning schema, the instructor would be asking only one learner at a time, and the acceptable response for an instructor would be either to probe the participant using other questions, provide more wait time, or offer her a way to save face like, "Who would you like to help you answer the question?" In a WILD HOG Questions scenario, the instructor has already planned to tell the participants, "Everyone, ask your elbow partner the same question and chat about your answers for one minute," because they want every participant to know the answer. As the instructor circulates, they can determine the level of understanding, correct errors within individual groups, and even create mini pullout groups to help targeted struggling learners without stopping learning for all learners.

In order to get a more accurate picture of what your learners know and can do, you want each of your participants to answer the questions when you check for understanding. Traditional instructors will feel that all the learners are at the same level if they can get one or two learners to respond appropriately. Not only is this an unwise assumption, it also sends the unintentional message to learners who are not prepared to go on, "I don't care if you don't understand, we are proceeding without you."

Since you want everyone to understand at the same level and be able to answer all the checking-for-understanding questions, it is best to elicit a whole-group response such as a hand gesture, a personal whiteboard, whiteboard marker on the desks, sticky posters, a communication device (electronic clickers, smartphones, or tablets), or choral response (everyone says the answer to the question at the same time as discussed in Section 13.4).

## Summary

1   Changing the mentality of whole-class questions is hard. We grew up with this, and this is how most of us were trained. Whole-class checking for understanding is a waste of our time and the learner's time. Engaging all learners is the best way to check for understanding.

2   A simple thumbs up or other gesture is often sufficient to give the instructor feedback on how they are doing. Partner questioning is powerful because learners hear, see, ask, and answer the questions.

3   When learners are struggling in traditional situations, an attentive instructor will stop instruction and help that learner. In WILD HOG prepared instruction, the instructor has the learners all asking the same questions and answering themselves.

## Questions to Consider

1   What am I going to do to plan questions for checking understanding so I know it really is time to move to the next topic?

_____

_____

_____

_____

2    What kind of question progression will I provide to partners to help them review what they have just learned in the current instruction?

_____

_____

_____

_____

_____

_____

_____

_____

_____

_____

_____

_____

_____

_____

_____

## Notes

1    Louis Pasteur and Alessandro Volta probably had many things in common. The one that most sticks out, though, is that they were scientists that discovered/invented things that now carry their names: pasteurization and the volt, as in unit of electricity (not Chevy Volt). By the way, Kermit the Frog and John the Baptist do have something in common . . . wait for it. . . . They have the same middle name (The).
2    Stoichiometry, using the concept of conservation of matter to determine proportions in chemical reactions, see www.britannica.com/science/stoichiometry

# 17

# Formative Questioning

## Constant Checking for Understanding That Doesn't Annoy

I looked at five different "expert" books on formative assessments, and some mentioned that the idea behind "formative" was to help the learner. Most viewed it as a process for instructors to get and give feedback. In my definition of formative assessment, it is all about the learner and learning. How did you learn to walk? The answer: real formative assessment. You fall and fall and fall, until you figure it out. You learn from your mistakes and try it again. That is the key, though: a formative assessment means you learn from your quiz, test, examination, or evaluation, and you do it again. That's what pilot training machines do. That's what nurse training robotic patients do. That's what computer simulations do. Why can't we do that in education? Rhetorical question. . . . We do formative assessments in "education," but we don't call it formative assessment. We call it a rough draft, a practice, a dry run, or a dress rehearsal.

## 17.1 Benefit to the Learner

Most educators I've encountered view formative assessments as a pretest or an introductory evaluation that is not graded. Some view formative assessments as intermediate quizzes and tests given between the big summative evaluations. Others feel it is a dipstick measurement of where the learners are and what adjustments the instructor needs to make to improve. It can be all of those, but I feel that they are all missing the true power of formative assessment: what it does for the learner.

The reason bowling is so fun is because we have many opportunities to try again.[4] Bowling is not easy: lifting that heavy ball, swinging it with only your fingers, figuring out how to schlep it down the alley without tripping, and then hurling it in the general direction of the pins. Real learning takes effort too, and, even more than bowling, it can be rewarding. A rough draft in writing is a perfect academic example of a formative assessment. The first time it is submitted, the instructor critiques it and gives it back. Each time, the learner corrects the mistakes and the product improves. When creating formative questions, the instructor needs to make sure that the learners understand the three main points in the following figure, and the instructor needs to follow the cycle with consistency in all instruction (see Figure 17.1).

Learners need to be able to:

◆ See what they are aiming at (a clear expectation)
◆ See immediately if their actions meet the target (detailed and timely feedback)
◆ Make corrections on their next turn (multiple opportunities for success).

Formative questions are just regular questions asked with a purpose and a method and then repeated. I introduced flashcards as explicit questions in Chapter 10. The power of flashcards is that you get to do them again after you make a mistake. In asking questions or, better yet, getting all of your learners asking questions, there needs to be a structure of what happens when the learner gets it wrong: they need to get the right, correct, or most appropriate

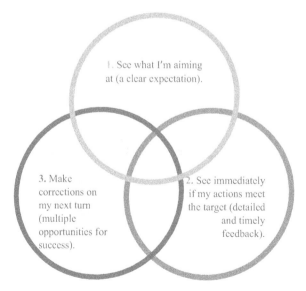

Figure 17.1 Learner Cycle of Formative Assessment and Improvement

answer, and they need an opportunity to show they learned from it by being able to repeat the activity. Back when I used to do whole-class questions and ask individuals using wait time, popsicle sticks, and timers, if a learner got a question wrong, I would always come back to that learner after the right answer had been given, in order to give that learner the opportunity to show they learned the answer. I was doing formative questioning and did not realize it. Formative assessment learning requires that there be multiple opportunities to take the assessment, quiz, evaluation, or test, with accurate feedback between each iteration. Each time they do it, more learning sticks, and they improve. How do you do formative questioning to engage all the learners? It is really not that different. Table 17.1 has some ideas.

**Table 17.1** Formative Feedback Loop

| Learner-Directed Formative Assessment | |
|---|---|
| **Who** | **What:** **In every case a set of questions is already prepared.** |
| Partner Questions—Elbow partners or find a partner. | Partners face off and each ask each other a question. If correct, it goes in the correct pile. If not, it goes in the pile to review. This is repeated until nothing is left in the review pile. |
| Small-Group Questions—four or five participants | Like partner questions, they choose elbow partners in the group, but after the partner work, the review piles of each partnership in the group are combined and then asked of the whole group, creating a new review pile until nothing is left in the review pile. |
| Targeted Group Questions— participants with similar needs | Questions are created specifically for the needs of the group: gifted, learning English, academically behind etc. Same process as small group questions. |
| Identity Groups Questions— participants who have similar likes— everyone who likes pineapple on pizza, those who like peperoni. . . . | Same as Small-Group Questions, but, after the group has eliminated its review pile, then new groups are formed with new identities and a new set of questions. |

| Response Group Questions-—participants who answered A, B, C, or D. Each group is one-quarter of the whole group. | This works with the four corners of the learning space. Learners who answered A in one corner, B in another corner, etc. It is similar to Identity Group Questions. A variation on this is low-tech; learners create an A, B, C, and D out of paper and each answer one of the four answer to the question. Personal whiteboards, clickers, or other technology do the same. |
|---|---|
| Silent Whole-Group Questions—the entire group | In this scenario, the answers to the questions are on the walls of the room, large enough to see from where they are standing. The instructor shows a written version of the questions and asks the questions, and the learners have to point to the answer. If they don't know the answer, they just have to look at where everyone else is pointing.[5] |
| Virtual Group Questions—the entire virtual group | In synchronous virtual teaching, all the learners could answer the question by doing hand signs, thumbs up/down, or writing the answer on a paper and holding it up to the camera. For asynchronous, simply responding to the question in the chat box where everyone can see each other's answers and respond to them too. |

The famous Rule of Three[6] states that *you cannot expect to learn something by just doing it once. You have to engage with the learning at least three times* (often more, see Chapter 11). All of the repetition does not have to happen the same day; as a matter of fact, it increases the likelihood of learning if it stretches over several days. One of the things I discovered as a Spanish instructor is that, if I asked the learners questions every day, eventually they would get it right. Before the start of each class, I stood by the door and shook every learner's hand. Before they could enter, I asked the learners a question that we had been working on. As the year progressed, I was able to ask almost any question to them in Spanish. If a learner struggled, the person behind them was able to help them out. What's even more interesting is that the learners enjoyed the one-on-one questions and viewed it as an exciting way to show what they knew.[7] Some instructors do this at the end of class as an "exit ticket."

## Summary

1   The idea of formative assessment is that through the actual assessment participants learn. The formative assessment must be a process and a cycle, not just done once. The process includes assessing learner knowledge, providing immediate feedback on the errors and how to fix them, and then providing other opportunities to take the same assessment. A rough draft is a perfect example of an effective formative assessment.

2   Formative assessments can be prepared for partners, small groups, and other specialty group configurations and follow the Rule of Three (or more). No formative learning occurs if the learners do not have a chance to do the exam, quiz, test, or evaluation over again.

## Questions to Consider

1   How will I use questions to help the learners learn from formative assessments?

_____

_____

_____

_____

2   Which type of group configuration most appeals to me?

_____

_____

_____

_____

3   What type of formative assessment question progression will I create?

_____

_____

_____

_____

_____

_____

_____

_____

_____

_____

_____

_____

_____

_____

_____

## Notes

1   We do all sorts of other kinds of alignment as well. If you have read any of Dr. Fenwick English's books or listened to his lectures, he forcefully drives home the point that we must have tight alignment with what we teach (the curriculum), how we teach it (the instruction), and what we test (state and local standards) (see http://soe.unc.edu/fac_research/faculty/english.php). So, as I stated earlier, we are basically in the alignment business because we spend tremendous amounts of time aligning curriculum with state and national standards. After that, we spend lots of time aligning what we teach to what we test. Then we align what we teach to how much students already know. We align what we teach to what the parents want and what the schoolboard wants. Finally, we align what we teach to what we want participants learn.

2   Most recently I wrote about the condors and capybaras that we all have in our classrooms and how to automatically differentiate for their needs (www.edutopia.org/blog/BTS-differentiation-for-all-students-ben-johnson). I have written two other articles for Edutopia.org that have to do with differentiation that you might be interested in also (www.edutopia.org/differentiated-instruction-active-learning) (www.edutopia.org/blog/differentiated-instruction-student-success).

3  For an interesting discussion about the gaps between what we know about education and what we do about it, read Howard Gardener's "What we do & don't know about learning" (found at www.jstor.org/discover/10.2307/20027891?uid=3739920&uid=2129&uid=2&uid=70&uid=4&uid=3739256&sid=21103013589691). He recounts the construction of a hypothetical museum of education. He chooses several consultants who would guide what gets put into the museum, and he illustrates what has changed over time in education and what has not. One thing he laments is that, while a lot is known about the brain and how it learns, not enough of that knowledge is actually put to use in the classroom. One of the obstacles to learning Gardener cites is that too many children are willing to believe in alternatives to evolution . . . hmmm.

4  I wrote a piece for Edutopia that explains how bowling is the best analogy for formative assessments. www.edutopia.org/formative-assessment-part-one and www.edutopia.org/formative-assessment-part-two.

5  This is a form of Total Physical Response that uses the brain-based research that the brain extends into the body, and, if the body is moving the right way, so is the brain. Here is an article I wrote on the subject: www.edutopia.org/blog/3-unused-teaching-tools-furniture-floors-and-walls-ben-johnson.

6  Read what I wrote about the Rule of Three in 2016: www.edutopia.org/blog/using-rule-three-learning-ben-johnson.

7  I wrote another piece about teaching to the test where I mentioned the entrance ticket. Enjoy: www.edutopia.org/blog/it-wrong-teach-test-ben-johnson.

# 18

# Pre-Post Test Mindset

## How to Use WILD HOG Questions as Evaluations

### 18.1 Value-Added Learning

I learned about the term "Value-Added Learning" in 2007. The idea was to determine a measure that would allow a school district to say that an instructor actually added value to their learners over the course of a year. In order to validate such a measure, learners were tested at the beginning of the year and then at the end of the year. If the progress exceeded the targeted learning mark, then the teacher was due for a bonus. The concept of determining progress through pre- and post-testing has been around long before teacher incentive grants came on the scene, and though the concept has merit, few instructors take advantage of it, primarily because it is another step to have to complete in an already hectic and busy profession.

Use the WILD HOG Questions that you prepared when you planned the instruction and create a short pretest. Administering this to the learners promotes several positive things. It gives the learners a pretty good idea of what they will be learning. It informs the learners what they know and what they don't know about the subject. It sets a baseline for everyone to know how much improvement was made, and it tells the instructor how to adjust the instruction to not waste time on what is already known.

As mentioned in the introduction to this section, it makes no sense to teach with one set of questions and test with another: they should be tightly aligned if we want to make learning easier on the participants. Jay McTighe and Grant Wiggins[1] rose to educational fame with the brilliant concept of creating the test (questions) before instruction in their book series *Understanding by Design* (2005).[2] Already having the questions created before instruction is the basis of WILD HOG Questions, and there is no reason, therefore, not to use those same questions on the examinations. Think of all the time you will save from having to remember all the questions that you asked and then write them for the examination! Since you already have a list of questions to pose to your learners in class, simply copy them directly to the test after the unit!

## 18.2  Teaching to the Test

"But that's teaching to the test!" some educators will complain. My answer to that is that if the test contains exactly what we want the learners to know and be able to do, then, yes, we should teach to the test.

If the pretest does not count toward a grade, there is a tendency for learners not to take the test seriously. One instructor came up with an ingenious method. The pretest and the posttest were the same. The pretest counted for the same as the posttest, but each question correctly answered on the pretest earned the learner one point extra credit to use on the posttest. After the posttest, the same score, including extra credit, was given to the pretest. Returning to the idea of Value-Added Testing, a powerful benefit of pre- and post-testing is that the learner can measure her own progress. Often this part is skipped due to time constraints, but it is well worth the time invested. It takes just a few seconds to give the learner their progress scores and praise them for their efforts, but it the learner will appreciate the encouragement. This data has tremendous value, especially for programs that are subject to enrollment fluctuations, but certainly as evidence in your resume; it is a powerful tool to be able to announce the amount of learning progress that was achieved under your instruction.

### Summary
1  Creation of WILD HOG Questions assures that the pretest and the posttest are aligned and that the learners will be prepared for success with no surprises.
2  Progress data will help the learner stay motivated and will bolster an instructor's confidence and resume.

### Questions to Consider
1  How will pre-testing improve learning effectiveness in my current instruction?

_____

_____

_____

2    How will I get my learners to take the pretest seriously?

_____

_____

_____

3    What will I do to follow up with pretest/posttest results with my learners?

_____

_____

_____

_____

_____

_____

## Notes

1    I interviewed Grant Wiggins and found him to be an intelligent and likeable person. Here is the interview: www.edutopia.org/blog/interview-grant-wiggins-power-backwards-design-ben-johnson. He passed away in 2015.
2    For the short explanation of *Understanding By Design*, see what Vanderbilt University prepared: https://cft.vanderbilt.edu/guides-sub-pages/understanding-by-design/. For the long version, here is a video; www.youtube.com/watch?v=4isSHf3SBuQ.

## Reference

McTighe, J., & Wiggins, G. (2005). *Understanding by design*. Alexandria, VA: Association of Supervisors and Curriculum Designers.

# 19

# Review and Retrench Questions

## What Do You Do When All of Your Participants Are Not Learning?

### 19.1 Don't Repeat the Same Mistakes

The stereotypical solution to someone not understanding you is to say the same thing again, but say it slower and louder. If a participant is struggling, there is no need to follow the same course of action that didn't work the first time but do it slower and louder. In helping my granddaughter with algebra, I discovered that she had some fundamental gaps in her knowledge about exponents. Rather than have her work through the study guide that her teacher gave her or have her watch the accompanying video where the teacher solves each problem, I asked her leading questions about what she knew about exponents (see Section 8.3 for more on leading questions). "If $a^2 = a \times a$, what is $a^3$?" When she seemed to understand the concept of exponents, then I asked questions on more difficult concepts, "If $a^2 \times a^3 = a^{(2+3)}$, then what is $a^3 \times a^5$?" One by one, I asked her leading questions in this fashion, until we had established a logical foundation in the law of exponents. With this new understanding, she was ready to tackle the review sheet her teacher had given her.

### 19.2 Affective Filter

I give this example to show that, in asking questions to review and retrench, it is much more productive to review and retrench what the participants do not know rather than what they do know, and the only way to find this out is to have them show you. I'm not suggesting that you call them up to the whiteboard, virtual display, or hologram projector and single them out. If the learners are not prepared, that would raise their affective filters—or fight or flight response—to a degree that cortisol will be released into their brains, effectively blocking any learning (memory). I had a misguided algebra instructor who did that under the guise of "teaching" and, to this day, I can remember the fear I had when I was called on, but could not tell you anything about the problem I was called to solve. To lower the affective filter, learners could work in pairs or small groups, while the instructor does two things 1) wanders around to keep everyone on task and 2) asks individuals questions to sample the learning of the groups.[1] What if an instructor finds that several learners are lacking the same knowledge? Quick targeted groups would be in order, and the instructor provides examples and asks leading questions to get them to understand the concepts. Once they get it, they go back to their groups. An instructor might have to do this several times in a review session. In this way, the learning for the entire group continues without interruption.

Often, small group games and competitions involving the base questions that the learner somehow did not retain help to fill in the gaps of learning. Flashcard reviews with partners also are powerful tools in filling in the gaps if done quickly (see Section 14.4).

## Summary
1 Often, simple leading questions are all that it takes to review and retrench to fill in learning gaps.
2 WILD HOG Questions designed for small groups are the perfect way to reduce embarrassment and the affective filter for struggling learners. Targeted mini lessons for learners with similar gaps in knowledge or understanding will help in the learning process.

## Questions to Consider
1 What will I do to identify struggling learners and help them fill in their knowledge or understanding gaps?

_____

_____

_____

2   Given my current instruction, what kind of leading question progression
    can I make to help struggling learners?

_____

_____

_____

_____

_____

_____

_____

_____

_____

_____

_____

_____

_____

_____

_____

_____

## Note

1   When I was a principal, one of my mantras to the teachers and aides was
    "If there are students in your classroom, you should be out helping them
    learn, not behind the desk. When students are not in your classroom, that
    is when you do paperwork, grade, and prepare materials."

# 20

## Formal Evaluations

### How Do You Construct Accurate Assessment Questions?

### 20.1 Sampling Learning

Formal evaluations are wonderful opportunities for learners to show what they know and what they can do with that knowledge. It is not formative. Learning is done. If your questioning skills have been up to snuff, each of your participants will feel prepared for the quiz or test. As you know, the assessment is a sampling of what the learners know and can do, and, as a summative expression of their knowledge, the assessment should be representative of the breadth of knowledge obtained, but it does not have to include every bit of knowledge, especially if the knowledge is the type that builds on other knowledge and skills, like math. For interim quizzes and tests, it is appropriate to emphasize vocabulary. But for end-of-unit or section assessments, to save time and to also communicate to the learners that the knowledge they have acquired needs to be put to use, I skip the simple vocabulary/definition questions, and, instead, I incorporate the vocabulary into application questions. They still will have to demonstrate a knowledge of the vocabulary in order to answer the questions.

### 20.2 WILD HOG Question Bank

Before instruction even begins, the first step in creating accurate assessment questions is to pull out your list of WILD HOG Questions and identify those questions that best represent the core knowledge and skills that best match the objectives. You may change one or two words to improve the questions, but they should be the same as the ones you frequently used in your instruction. The assessment is not the time to insert questions that the participants have not seen multiple times already (remember the Rule of Three?). The second step is to review those questions to make sure that there is no ambiguity about what the answer should be. The final step is for you to decide the format of the questions, remembering that you will have to grade them. What I mean by that is that if you create an assessment that is all essay answers, then you will have to read each one and make a determination if the question was answered completely. My general philosophy was that I would rather spend my time in the knowledge acquisition part of the learning cycle than in the knowledge demonstration part.

## 20.3  Performance-Based Evaluations

I made my quizzes so that the learners could exchange papers and grade them themselves, and the larger tests were part performance-based and part knowledge based. The performance-based portion, in my case, was having a conversation with the learners in Spanish. In math it might be an explanation on how to utilize the quadratic equation to predict the arrivals of airplanes at certain destinations for connecting flights. For philosophy, it might be a comparative treatise on John Locke and Henry David Thoreau. In English it could be a five-paragraph persuasive essay. For a first-grade classroom it could be to create a piece of art that shows what they learned about the moon, and so on. The knowledge portion of the tests could be primarily multiple-choice answers. For tests under a tight timeframe, matching and true/false questions can be added.

## 20.4  Accurate Multiple Choice

The process of creating accurate tests from your Wild Hog Questions means that the answers on the multiple choice need to reflect what was learned also. Typically, educators, curriculum developers, and psychometricians create multiple-choice answers in the following way: One answer is easily identifiable as the incorrect answer. One answer is the correct answer, and the remaining two could be simply modifications of the correct answer or misleading similar answers based on misconceptions of the correct answer. If you are like me, this is the most frustrating part of taking a multiple-choice test: trying to determine if you take the answer on face value, or if the answer is saying something deeper alluding to the truth. Often, the test-maker feels that the correct answer is too obvious and changes the phraseology or the vocabulary to disguise the correct answer. I will be blunt. None of this helps learning, and it in fact skews the results of the evaluations, as well as alienating the very people we are supposed to be helping to learn. I propose that no answer choice on the test or quiz should be new. Each answer choice in a multiple-choice question, especially the correct one, should be something with which the learners are familiar enough to make a valid distinction. There is no need to trick or trap learners into making incorrect selections (see Table 20.1).

**Table 20.1**  Creating Effective Multiple Choice Questions

**Effective Multiple Choice Questions**

| *Poor Questions*[1] | **Reason it's bad** | **Better questions** |
| --- | --- | --- |
| *Thoreau's experiment was to "live deliberately, to front only the essential facts of life, and see if I could not learn what it had to teach, and not, when I came to die, discover that I had not lived."* | Obviously true— too much detail to not be true. | Thoreau's experiment was to "live deliberately, to front only the essential facts of life." |
| *Thoreau inspired the 20th-century protest movements with his "civil disobedience," later protest movements against the Vietnam War..* | Confusing and incomplete sentence— obviously false. | Thoreau inspired the protest movements against the Vietnam War with his "civil disobedience." |
| *With regard to God, Locke asserts*<br>*A) That God does not exist*<br>*B) That God exists but cannot be known*<br>*C) That certainty of God's existence can be known through intuition*<br>*D) That certainty of God's existence can only be known through faith*<br>*E) That certainty of God's existence can be known through observation* | Choices C and E are not mutually exclusive like the rest, meaning one of them is the correct answer. The author says C is the correct answer. | Locke believed: (choose only one)<br>A) That God cannot exist<br>B) That God exists but cannot be known<br>C) That certainty of God's existence can only be known through intuition<br>D) That certainty of God's existence can only be known through faith<br>E) That certainty of God's existence can only be known through observation |

## Effective Multiple Choice Questions

| | | |
|---|---|---|
| Consent is:<br>A) Something has an unappealing odor<br>B) When you approve something or allow something to take place<br>C) Refusing to do something<br>D) When you write your name | The longest answer is the correct one, B. | According to Locke, consent is:<br>A) Something that smells bad.<br>B) When you approve of something<br>C) Refusing to do something<br>D) When you write your name |
| According to John Locke, your natural rights include . . .<br>A) Education, privacy, and security<br>B) Clothing, food, and shelter<br>C) Freedom, work, and protection<br>D) Life, liberty, and property | A, B, and C are too similar. Anyone familiar at all with the Declaration of Independence would know that D is the correct answer. | According to John Locke, your natural rights include:<br>A) First, second, and third amendments<br>B) Life, liberty, and pursuit of happiness.<br>C) Freedom, labor, and protection<br>D) Life, liberty, and property |
| John Locke said that an agreement to make a government and follow its laws is known as a<br>A) Natural agreement<br>B) Social contract<br>C) Constitution<br>D) Declaration of intent | While the author was seeking a particular answer, any one of the four could answer the question. The correct answer was B. | John Locke said that an agreement to form a government and then follow its laws is known as a<br>A) Social Agreement<br>B) Social Contract<br>C) Social Constitution<br>D) Social Compact |
| Which of the following is not true about Gottfried Leibniz (There is only one answer. Read carefully)<br>A) He was credited with developing calculus<br>B) He developed a theory of elemental atoms that he called "monads"<br>C) He sought to explain why we have a "universe" instead of a "multiverse"<br>D) He divided causes into proximate and immediate causes<br>E) He divided reasons into efficient and sufficient reasons<br>F) He taught that all monads and their interrelatedness were ultimately orchestrated by God | The directions are confusing. The author repeats phrases to confuse the learner. The untruth is D—"Multiverse" is a modern word,[2] so I would have chosen C and gotten it wrong. | Which of the following is not true about Gottfried Leibniz (choose one)?<br>A) He was credited with developing calculus<br>B) He developed a theory of elemental atoms that he called "monads"<br>C) He sought to explain why we have only one universe<br>D) He divided causes into proximate and immediate causes |

**Summary**

1   Since you already have a list of questions prepared before instruction, there is nothing preventing you from making the examination at the same time.
2   The questions on the examination should be the same questions used in learning and the same questions provided in the pretest.
3   Not all of the WILD HOG Questions should be used on the examination, only the most important ones.
4   Good multiple-choice questions are not meant to trick the learner but to allow him to discriminate clearly the right answer.

**Questions to Consider**

1   Which WILD HOG Questions in my current instruction are the most important to put on an evaluation?

_____

_____

_____

_____

_____

_____

_____

_____

_____

_____

_____

_____

_____

2   How do I change these questions to include fair multiple-, choice answers?

_____

_____

_____

_____

_____

_____

_____

_____

_____

_____

_____

_____

_____

_____

_____

## Notes

1    Taken from the site: www.proprofs.com/quiz-school/browse, where you can make your own quiz and take many others. It creates a fancy certificate suitable for framing when you are done.

2    In 1895, William James, an American philosopher, coined the word "multiverse," and DC Comics began using it in 1944 with Wonder Woman and Mr. Mxyzptlk, a universe-hopping trickster. Since then it has been a staple in Marvel and DC Comics as well as the new _Star Trek_ with Chris Pine.

# Section IV

## Assessing Learning Conclusion

The section on assessment was almost anti-climactic, wasn't it? The hard work of questioning had already been done.

The creation of WILD HOG Questions at the beginning of the planning process makes the creation of formative, pretest, posttest, and formal evaluations easy to create before instruction begins. Take a few minutes and create your learning plan for what you want to continue learning. Don't forget to look at the end notes for each chapter for additional sources of learning that you may want to include in your plan.

Section IV  Assessing Learning Professional Growth Plan

| Professional Growth Activity | Resources Needed | Due Date |
|---|---|---|
| 1. Checking for Understanding |  |  |
|  |  |  |
|  |  |  |
| 2. Formative Questioning |  |  |
|  |  |  |
|  |  |  |

| Professional Growth Activity | Resources Needed | Due Date |
|---|---|---|
| 3. Pre-Post Test Mindset | | |
| | | |
| | | |
| 4. Review and Retrench Questions | | |
| | | |
| | | |
| 5. Formal Evaluations | | |
| | | |
| | | |

# Index

For Product Safety Concerns and Information please contact our EU
representative  GPSR@taylorandfrancis.com
Taylor & Francis Verlag GmbH, Kaufingerstraße 24, 80331 München, Germany